CIVIL WAR COMMANDERS

CIVIL WAR COMMANDERS

FROM FORT SUMTER TO APPOMATTOX COURT HOUSE

Chester G. Hearn • Rick Sapp • Steven M. Smith

M

METRO BOOKS
NEW YORK

© 2008 by Compendium
Publishing Ltd.

This 2008 edition published by
Metro Books, by arrangement with
Compendium Publishing Ltd.

THE AUTHORS
Chester G. Hearn is a former member of
the United States armed forces. He has
written several books on U.S. military
history, three of which have been "alter-
nate selections" for the History Book Club
of America.
Rick Sapp, the son of a Yankee mother
and a Confederate father, is a former
magazine and newspaper editor and the
author of fifteen books, as well as
hundreds of magazine articles, from
history to cycling to enjoying the outdoors,
Steven M. Smith founded Sarpedon
Publishers in 1991, specializing in military
history titles. He has written a number of
books, edited far more, across a range of
eras from Alexander the Great to the U.S.
invasion of Iraq. His most recent book is
The Stonewall Brigade (2008).

Project Manager: Ray Bonds
Designer: Cara Rogers
Color Reproduction:
Anorax Imaging Ltd

Metro Books
122 Fifth Avenue
New York, NY 10011

ISBN-13: 978-1-4351-0396-2
ISBN-10: 1-4351-0396-3

Printed and bound in China

1 3 5 7 9 10 8 6 4 2

Contents

Page 1: Ulysses S. Grant, one of the greatest commanders in American history.

Previous pages: At Antietam shortly after America's bloodiest single day, President Abraham Lincoln cuts a towering figure among his commanders.

Left: Feared and hated in the South, the Union's William Tecumseh Sherman predicted and fought a long and bloody war.

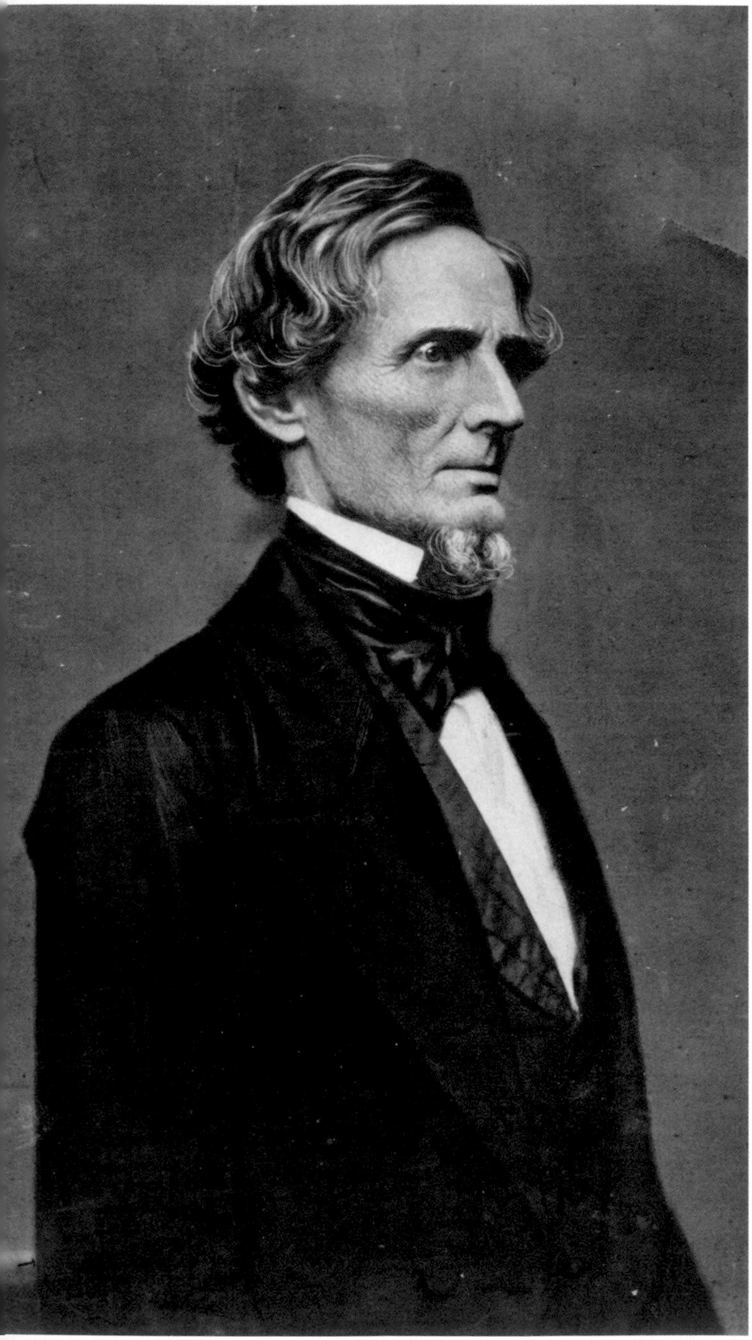

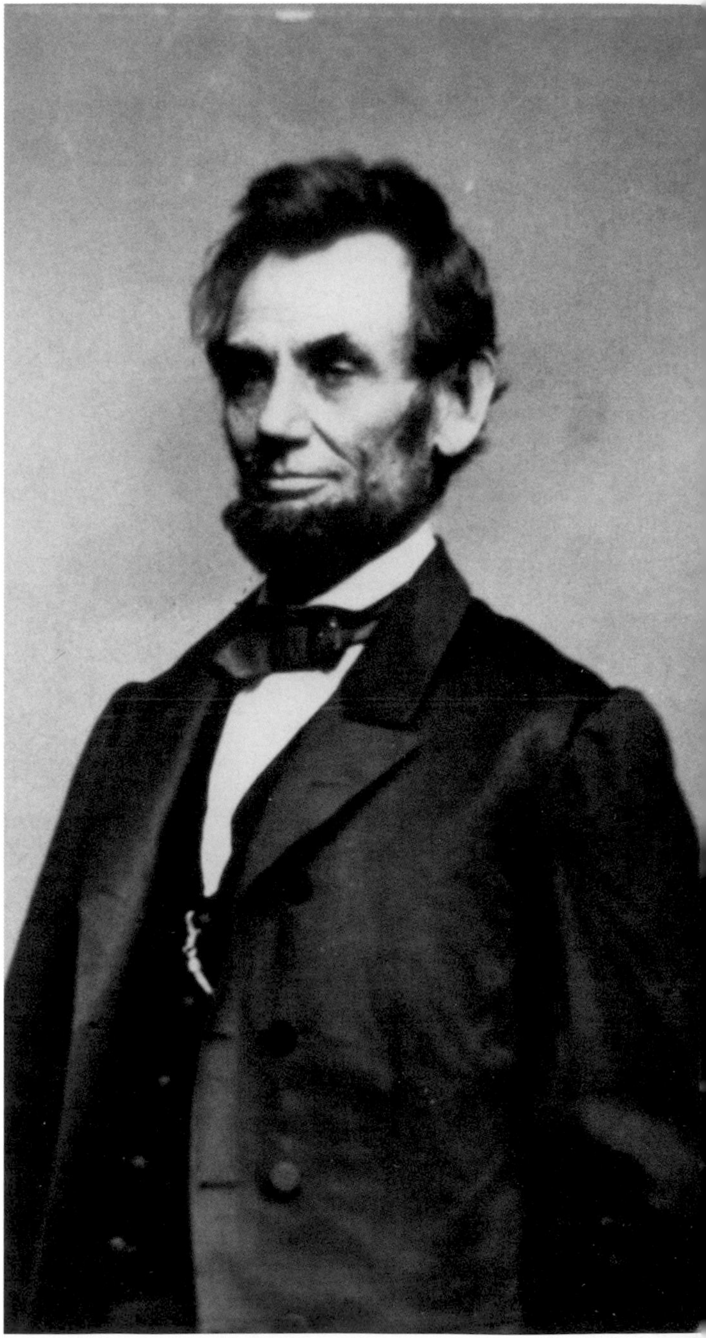

Introduction

The Civil War, in terms of casualties by far the costliest war in American history, propelled men from all walks of life into sudden prominence. Many of them forged their names in lasting glory—frequently through their deaths in battle—while others were branded as goats or failures. Far many others emerged from the war with greater success than they could ever have seen had the conflict not happened, and went on to become some of America's most honored citizens.

As opposed to a war between foreign nations, for which every power is more or less prepared, the War Between the States erupted at close quarters, with neither side expecting the ferocity, size, and duration of the conflict. At the start of 1861, the United States possessed an army of about 15,000 men, most of whom were west of the Mississippi fighting Indians or garrisoning California. A few others were in island forts or batteries facing the Atlantic Ocean should the British ever return. Though tensions between North and South had been festering for years, few, if any, citizens expected all-out war, and those who did thought it would be over quickly with one great battle.

What was least expected was the utter determination of each side, and the fact that within the next four years, 3,000,000 men would be put under arms to contest the issue of Southern secession. Given this explosion of soldiers, a multitude of officers was also necessary to lead them, and the result was a plethora of famous commanders that we still honor today.

Though unprepared for war, the United States did not totally lack for trained officers, as its Military Academy at West Point had been training young men for decades, and many of these had tasted combat in the Mexican War or against Indians. Of over 1,100 West Point graduates available for duty in the Civil War, some 300 went with the Confederacy, the rest remaining with the Union. Naturally both sides looked to these men first, and the majority of senior commanders throughout the conflict were West Point graduates.

A second strata of commanders was drawn from local community leaders, often successful businessmen or politicians. These were proven leaders in the civilian sphere who were able to transfer their talents to recruiting volunteers into regiments and afterward leading them into

Left: The political leaders—Jefferson Davis (1808–1889) and Abraham Lincoln (1809–1865)—while both born in Kentucky, hailed from different backgrounds. Davis was a graduate of West Point and fought in the Mexican-American War before becoming secretary of war. He was elected president of the Confederate States of America and was sworn in on February 18, 1862. He held that position throughout the Civil War, relying on few advisers and interfering far more than Lincoln did in the actual operations of his armies. Lincoln, on the other hand, was a civilian, a lawyer, who had no military experience, but whose choice of Edwin M. Stanton as secretary of war (replacing Simon Cameron in 1862) through to the end of the war was a resounding success. Lincoln searched for three years for a general who would lead his armies to victory; he eventually found Grant, and happily bowed out of military affairs almost entirely. Five days after Lee's surrender, Lincoln was shot dead in a theater by an actor and Confederate sympathizer, John Wilkes Booth.

Left: General Grant (seated, third from left) with eight members of his staff, including (second from right) Colonel Ely S. Parker, who wrote out the terms of surrender that Grant demanded for the ceremony at Appomattox Court House.

battle. Politics played a role, as state governors both North and South, as well as the respective administrations in Washington and Richmond, wished to reward their most influential supporters with high positions.

The phenomenon of "political generals," however, was most prevalent in the North, as Lincoln sat on shaky ground as the country's first Republican president, and furthermore faced a re-election during the war. Men like John McClernand and Nathaniel Banks were "war Democrats," who, along with their constituencies, Lincoln wished to draw close to his side. Confederate president Davis, though not immune to political infighting, did not have to face an election, and as a West Point graduate himself, and former secretary of war, was able to be more hard-headed in his appointments of officers.

A third strata of commanders emerged completely by surprise, consisting of men who simply volunteered out of patriotism and proved to be excellent combat leaders. The North's Joshua Chamberlain and the South's Patrick Cleburne were prototypes of this kind. Due to its larger army and vast duties occupying territory, the Union had more room to experiment with commanders than did the Confederacy, which more needed men who could win battles. With his allegiance to West Point training, Jefferson Davis was slow to realize the worth of pure combat talents such as Nathan Bedford Forrest, perhaps the best pure fighter of the war. At the same time, however, the West Pointers around Lincoln, from Halleck to Grant and Sherman, made no bones about their contempt for "amateurs," including McClernand, Banks, and the bombastic politician-turned-soldier, Ben Butler.

Command assignments in the Civil War could be had

by various ways, but promotion, as a rule, could be gained only on the battlefield. Since the Union gradually won the war, some of its commanders were able to claim success from the benefit of superior numbers and resources; on the Confederate side, visible courage was required in order to command troops. In 1863 a British officer in the

Below: Grant holds a "council of war" at Massaponax Church, Virginia, on May 21, 1864.

Right: Just sixteen years old when the Civil War broke out, Galusha Pennypacker volunteered for the 9th Pennsylvania Infantry and a few weeks later formed a new company that became part of the 97th Pennsylvania. He was just seventeen when promoted to major, and still only twenty when he became brigadier general—the youngest in American history and still too young even to vote for the president who appointed him. Wounded eight times during the war, he was awarded the Medal of Honor for his courageous performance during the assault on Fort Fisher.

Confederate service commented to a countryman, "Every atom of authority has to be purchased by a drop of your blood." Though good commanders were sometimes passed over for promotion, due to personal squabbles or other factors, it can be said that both Lincoln and Davis were constantly on the lookout for men who could successfully fight.

Both the Union and Confederate armies had similar command structures, as would be expected since they were all trained the same way. Colonels commanded regiments, brigadier generals brigades, and major generals divisions. There it differs because the Confederacy named its corps commanders lieutenant generals, whereas the Union named only one during the war: Grant, who was by then supreme commander of all Union forces. The Federals chose the system of designating "Major General Commanding Corps" or "Commanding Army" for their higher ranks; thus every leader of the Army of the Potomac was no more than a major general, though he faced several lieutenant generals on the other side. The Confederates designated their commanders above corps, including Robert E. Lee, as simply "General," though often described as "Full General."

The system of ranking lieutenant generals above major generals derives from a British precedent dating back to the Restoration, in which the ranks were Captain General, Lieutenant General, and Sergeant-Major General. Over time the word "sergeant" (as well as "captain") dropped out, leaving lieutenant outranking major. The Federals, as a rule, named their armies after rivers (the Potomac, Cumberland, Tennessee, Ohio, Mississippi, James, etc.), while the Confederates chose

Right: Troops led by Union General Alfred H. Terry during the attack on Fort Fisher, North Carolina, January 15, 1865. There were disproportionate casualties among commanders, especially those who led their men into battle

Left: Ropes stashed on shore helped gunboats and transport vessels get through rough areas of rivers, such as here, on the Tennessee. Federal forces generally named their armies after rivers (for example, the Army of the Tennessee), while the Confederates chose states and territories (Army of Tennessee).

states. Thus, for example, the Army of Tennessee under Bragg, Johnston, and Hood is not to be confused with the Federal Army of *the* Tennessee, under Grant, Sherman, and McPherson.

When examining the most prominent commanders of the Civil War, one is struck by how much danger they faced, no matter how exalted their rank. In fact, by way of setting an example to their men in the terrifying ordeal of combat, commanders frequently ran an even greater risk than the rank and file by standing out front and leading their men. Casualties were most prevalent among brigade commanders, but during the Civil War era, when firearms technology had approached, but not quite reached, beyond-the-horizon capability (including in naval warfare), everyone in a battle was at risk.

A total of sixty-five Union generals died during the war (out of 583), while ninety-two Confederate generals (out of 425) failed to survive the conflict. At the South's height, Robert E. Lee commanded an extraordinary group of corps commanders in the Army of Northern Virginia; but by the time the war had finished, Stonewall Jackson, Jeb Stuart, and A. P. Hill were dead, while Longstreet and Ewell had been crippled. On the Northern side, one need only look to Gettysburg where, among corps commanders, Reynolds was killed on the first day, Sickles wounded on the second, and Hancock shot on the third.

The manner of commanders' deaths varied widely, from the Union's John Sedgwick being killed by a sharpshooter (after famous last words, "They couldn't hit an elephant at this distance.") to Pat Cleburne's demise at the head of his troops at Franklin (where some say he was riddled by fifty bullets; others say only one through the heart). The commander of the Federal Army of the Tennessee, James McPherson, died alone, after being shot by a Confederate skirmisher, as did A. S. Johnston at Shiloh, who bled to death quietly after having dispatched his surgeon to attend to Federal wounded.

The great death toll among Civil War commanders need not disguise the record of their wounds, which were suffered frequently, and in some cases repeatedly. Ranging from Sherman's nick in the hand at Shiloh to Hood's loss of an arm and a leg at, respectively, Gettysburg and Chickamauga, it was a rare commander who was not hit at least once in the war. Knowing this, Confederate troops repeatedly kept Robert E. Lee out of combat, shouting "Lee to the rear" and refusing to advance when their commander impulsively sought to join them in attacks. With just a week to go until Appomattox, commanders such as Sheridan were still exposing themselves to fire, while Forrest, in the west, was busy fending off saber thrusts by an ill-fated Union officer.

In the Civil War, as in all other wars, many of the most courageous commanders may have died during the first clashes, without time for their experiences to enter the annals of history. With apologies to the heroes on both sides whose stories have not been told, herein is an attempt to recognize those whose record is evident. Many survived the war and others did not, but these concise essays are meant to describe their combined experiences, their gallantry and sacrifices that typified all ranks during the War Between the States.

Adams, William Wirt

(1819–1888) Confederate
Senior position: Brigade commander, Army of
Mississippi
Final rank: Brigadier

Wirt Adams formed the 1st Mississippi Cavalry at the start of the Civil War, and in September 1863 was promoted to brigade command. Operating mainly in Mississippi, he fought in the battles around Vicksburg, chased Grierson's raiders, and contested Sherman's march on Meridien. Adams' command was typical of Confederate cavalry units that could be roused to fierce defense of their home states but lacked the discipline necessary for broader operations.

Above: Wirt Adams and his command acted largely alone in central Mississippi, as the main focus of the war shifted elsewhere.

Alexander, Edward Porter

(1835–1910) Confederate
Senior position: Corps artillery commander, Army of
Northern Virginia
Final rank: Brigadier General

Born in Washington, Georgia, Alexander became one of only three officers in the Confederate army to attain the rank of brigadier general of artillery. He resigned from the U.S. Army on May 1, 1861, and received an appointment in the Confederate service as captain of engineers. He served as General Beauregard's signal officer during First Manassas, after which he became chief of ordnance for the Army of Northern Virginia. While serving as chief of artillery under General Longstreet, Alexander received promotion to brigadier general.

Alexander participated in all the early battles and in

Above: After the war, Alexander wrote one of the most incisive memoirs of the Civil War, "Fighting for the Confederacy."

almost every campaign of the Army of Northern Virginia. In May 1863 he took part in Stonewall Jackson's flanking assault on General Hooker's Union lines at Chancellorsville. During the third day of fighting at Gettysburg, he commanded 140 cannon. After conducting a two-hour bombardment on Cemetery Hill, he observed that General Pickett had not advanced, and wrote a hurried message, "If you are coming at all you must come at once, or I cannot give you proper support." When in 1863 Longstreet joined General Bragg to participate in the Tennessee campaign, Alexander took his artillery south for operations at Chickamauga and Knoxville.

During the campaigns of 1864 in Virginia, he took part in the battles of Spotsylvania, Cold Harbor, and Petersburg. He also warned of mining operations among the Petersburg trenches and urged countermining. Shortly after the battle of the Crater, Alexander sustained a serious wound that kept him out of action until a few months before General Lee's withdrawal from Petersburg. On April 9, 1865, Alexander surrendered at Appomattox and obtained his parole. Returning to civilian life, he led a distinguished career as a professor of engineering at South Carolina University. Later he became active in railroads and the oil industry and held several public offices.

Above: The 600-yard Mahone Mine, discovered after the siege of Petersburg, April 1865.

Anderson, Richard Heron

(1821–1879) Confederate
Senior position: Corps commander, Army of Northern Virginia
Final rank: Lieutenant General

Called "Fightin' Dick" by his associates, Anderson became one of Robert E. Lee's most trusted generals. While commanding a brigade from South Carolina, he became part of the Army of Northern Virginia. Under Lee, Anderson commanded a division from the Peninsula to Chancellorsville and after the battle of the Wilderness earned promotion to lieutenant general as a corps commander. Once, after repulsing several assaults, Lee shook his hand, and said, "My noble soldier, I thank you from the bottom of my heart."

Above: Anderson had to fill formidable shoes when taking over the Army of Northern Virginia's First Corps.

17

Anderson, Robert
(1805–1871) Federal
Senior position: Commander, Department of the
Cumberland
Final rank: Brigadier General

Armistead, Lewis Addison
(1817–1863) Confederate
Senior position: Brigade commander, Army of Northern
Virginia
Final rank: Brigadier General

Anderson is best remembered as a major when in April 1861 he defended Fort Sumter against a thirty-four-hour bombardment from Confederate shore batteries in the Charleston, South Carolina, harbor. Although he surrendered the fort on April 13, he emerged a hero. Shortly afterward, President Lincoln elevated Anderson to the permanent rank of brigadier general.

Above: Anderson won national fame at Fort Sumter, but was unable to retain high command afterward.

Although dismissed from West Point for breaking a plate over the head of Jubal Early, Armistead followed a military career. A Virginia native, Armistead distinguished himself while fighting in every major battle of the Army of Northern Virginia until Gettysburg. While leading a brigade during Pickett's charge, he fell mortally wounded assaulting the crest of Cemetery Hill.

Above: Armistead's death in Pickett's Charge, sword holding his hat overhead, is one of the iconic images of the war.

Ashby, Turner

(1828–1862) Confederate
Senior position: Brigade commander, Army of Northern Virginia
Final rank: Brigadier General

Baird, Absalom

(1824–1905) Federal
Senior position: Division commander, Army of the Cumberland
Final rank: Major General

A natural leader and a gifted horseman from Virginia, Ashby commanded Stonewall Jackson's cavalry during the famous Shenandoah Valley campaign in the spring of 1862. His scouting ability and intrepid fighting skills marked him as one of the brilliant cavalry leaders of the war. He died holding back Union forces near Harrisonburg.

Above: No cavalry leader earned such a reputation in so short a time as Turner Ashby.

Baird served on many fields, both as a staff officer and a line officer from the Battle of Manassas to the final capitulation of Confederate forces in North Carolina. As a division commander he served under Rosecrans, Thomas, and Sherman. During the Battle of Jonesboro, Georgia, in September 1864, he earned the Medal of Honor for collapsing the enemy's position.

Above: Baird postwar, belying the dynamism with which we fought in both the Western and Eastern theaters.

Banks, Nathaniel Prentiss

(1816–1894) Federal
Senior position: Commander,
Department of the Gulf
Final rank: Major General

Banks' education began when he went to work as a boy in a cotton mill superintended by his father. He labored hard to become a politician and in 1853 was elected Speaker of the House of Representatives and in 1858 governor of Massachusetts. Banks had a brilliant mind, which President Lincoln attempted to employ in a military capacity by promoting him to major general.

During his brief military career as a field general, Banks led his forces into some of the worst defeats of the Civil War. Even West Point generals commanding his divisions could not keep Banks from making mistakes. Stonewall Jackson drove him out of the Shenandoah Valley during the spring of 1862 and in August defeated him again at Cedar Mountain. Sent by Lincoln to Louisiana, Banks captured Port Hudson in 1863 but suffered

Left: Banks was the prototype of a Union "political" general, and though personally brave was repeatedly beaten on the battlefield by Stonewall Jackson and others.
Right: The Federals' siege of Port Hudson on the Mississippi lasted forty-eight days, from May 21 to July 9, 1863. Banks was repulsed at least twice before the Confederate stronghold surrendered on hearing of Vicksburg's capitulation.

enormous casualties. When given command of the Red River expedition, Banks demonstrated his lack of military skill by completely bungling the campaign. Although Congress thanked Banks for having "skill, courage, and endurance which compelled the surrender of Port Hudson," the gesture was politically motivated. When Banks mustered out of the service in August 1865, Massachusetts immediately sent him back to Congress, where he served six terms.

Barksdale, William

(1821–1863) Confederate
Senior position: Brigade commander, Army of Northern Virginia
Final rank: Brigadier General

Bate, William B.

(1826–1905) Confederate
Senior position: Division commander, Army of Tennessee
Final rank: Major General

Although born in Tennessee, Barksdale commanded the 13th Mississippi at First Manassas. He distinguished himself on every field of battle while leading his sharp-shooters, known as "Barksdale's Mississippians." On the second day of Gettysburg, he suffered a mortal wound during the assault of the divisions of Hood and McLaw on the Round Tops.

Bate began his military career as colonel of the 2nd Tennessee Infantry. After recovering from a wound at Shiloh, he became a brigadier general and fought at Tullahoma and Chickamauga. He distinguished himself at Chattanooga, earned promotion to major general, and afterwards fought in every battle from Georgia to the final surrender at Greensboro, North Carolina.

Above: At Fredericksburg, Barksdale's Mississippi sharpshooters held off the Army of the Potomac for a day.

Above: Bate lost control of his troops during Hood's 1864 invasion of Tennessee. At Nashville they were the first to break.

Beauregard, Pierre Gustave Toutant

(1818–1893) Confederate
Senior position: Commander, Army of Mississippi
Final rank: General

Beauregard earned the distinction of firing the first shots of the Civil War on April 12, 1861, when he bombarded Fort Sumter. On July 21, 1861, he earned further distinction by winning the Civil War's first major battle at First Manassas, though much of the credit went to Joseph E. Johnston. Being vain and egotistical, Beauregard always wanted all the credit. Despite being raised to full general, he habitually disagreed with Jefferson Davis and paid the price for his unguarded insolence.

Placed second in command to General Albert Sidney Johnston, he assumed command of the Army of Tennessee after Johnston's death at Shiloh. After retiring to Corinth and holding back General Henry Halleck's massive Union force, Beauregard became ill. Davis took advantage of Beauregard's sick leave and replaced him with Braxton Bragg. When Beauregard cried foul, Davis assigned him to a defensive role at Charleston, South Carolina. Beauregard served ably there, and in May 1864 probably saved Richmond by bottling up General Benjamin Butler's Army of the James at Bermuda Hundred. In early 1865, as Union General, Sherman began his campaign in the

Top: Beauregard won the war's first real battle for the Confederates, Bull Run (First Manassas), July 21, 1861.

Above: A senior Confederate commander, Beauregard was always considered as fanciful as he was brilliant.

Carolinas, Beauregard joined forces with Joseph Johnston's army and surrendered on April 18, 1865.

Bee, Barnard Elliott

(1824–1861) Confederate
Senior position: Brigade commander, Army of Northern Virginia
Final rank: Brigadier General

Bragg, Braxton

(1817–1876) Confederate
Senior position: Commander, Army of Tennessee
Final rank: General

A South Carolinian, Bee fought his first big Civil War battle at First Manassas on July 21, 1861, and died the next day. He commanded a brigade under Joe Johnston and made his stand on Henry House Hill. With his brigade suffering from severe fire, he created a legend by referring to Thomas J. Jackson as standing "like a stone wall" in the face of heavy fire.

Above: An example of how the brave die first, Bee is best remembered for giving "Stonewall" his name.

Born in Warrenton, North Carolina, Bragg went to West Point at a time when military tactics relied on muskets, bayonets, and smoothbore cannon. Those same implements were prevalent when as a young officer Bragg fought in the Seminole Wars and on the frontier. During the Mexican War he earned three brevets as an artillery

Above: Bragg led an excellent army but failed to achieve the decisive victories Lee did in Virginia.

captain. At Buena Vista, when General Zachary Taylor wanted more grapeshot fired at the enemy, he hollered at Bragg, his favorite artillerist, and said, "Double shot those guns and give 'em hell!"

Bragg retired from the army in 1856 as a lieutenant colonel to run his Louisiana plantation but in early 1861 rejoined the military as a major general in the militia. After becoming president of the Confederacy, Jefferson Davis called for 75,000 volunteers and appointed Bragg brigadier general in the Provisional Army of the Confederate States. Although given a small command at Pensacola and Mobile, Bragg enjoyed

Above: A scene from the Hornet's Nest at Shiloh, where Union troops temporarily held off the surprise Rebel onslaught.

a favorable working relationship with Davis.

Elevated to major general on September 12, Bragg assumed command of Albert Sidney Johnston's

II Corps. At Shiloh on the morning of April 6, Bragg fought his first big battle of the war. He sent the II Corps against the Federal left, which resulted in a bloody contest at the "hornet's nest" that lasted more than five hours. He rushed regiments forward to seal gaps in brigades and fought off several counterattacks. When General Johnston consulted with Bragg, the two generals decided on a foolish bayonet charge. Johnston sustained a mortal wound, and Beauregard assumed command. The fighting resumed on April 7. When Beauregard sent Bragg an order, the latter replied, "The battle is lost."

Befriending Davis paid another dividend. The president advanced Bragg to general to rank from April 6 and on June 27 put him in command of the Army of Tennessee after Beauregard became ill. Despite leading an abortive invasion into

Above: Bragg lost 21,000 men during the Battle of Chickamauga, Georgia, September 19/20, 1863.

Kentucky in August 1862, which ended in a repulse at Perryville, Bragg retained command and retired into Tennessee.

After a virtual competition to see which force could move the slowest, the Army of the Cumberland under Major General William S. Rosecrans collided with Bragg's Army of Tennessee at Stones River

Below: Bragg defeated Rosecrans' Union forces at Chickamauga, September 19–20, 1863, the Confederates' only real victory in the western theater.

(Murfreesboro) on December 31, 1862. While neither army demonstrated any appetite for demolishing the other, Bragg at least initiated the assault and turned back Rosecrans' line. Bragg became confused and failed to follow up his advantage, and

on January 3 he ordered a retreat. Rosecrans claimed victory but failed to pursue Bragg, who retired with his army in tact. Bragg used his infantry to block the roads to Chattanooga and his cavalry to disrupt Rosecrans' communications.

For the next six months Davis remained tolerant of Bragg's inactivity, but Lincoln became annoyed at Rosecrans' reluctance to fight. On June 26 Rosecrans completely deceived Bragg and struck the Confederates at Tullahoma, Tennessee. Bragg never properly organized his forces, and though holding a good defensive position, he retired on June 30, destroyed the bridges over the Tennessee River, occupied Chattanooga, and set the stage for the Chickamauga campaign.

In early September 1863, Rosecrans maneuvered Bragg out of Chattanooga and occupied the city. Bragg moved his army into northwest Georgia and developed a strong defensive position along Chickamauga Creek. Prodded by President Lincoln to finish off Bragg's army, Rosecrans moved into Georgia in mid-August at the same time that Bragg drew reinforcements from other fields. Bragg intended to maul the Federal right and reoccupy Chattanooga. When the fighting began on September 19, Bragg struck the Federal lines in a series of sledgehammer blows. Rosecrans blundered in arranging his troops, which enabled Confederates to pour through every Federal position but the one held by Major General George Thomas's corps. The rest of Rosecrans' army fled back to Chattanooga led by two corps commanders and the general himself. Bragg followed without attacking Chattanooga, but he surrounded the city and cut Federal communications.

Bragg dallied too long. After being defeated by General Grant in November 1863, Bragg asked to be relieved. Davis brought him to Richmond and placed him in charge of "the conduct of the military operations in the armies of the Confederacy." By this appointment Davis irritated other generals because he made Bragg technically superior to his peers but junior by virtue of the date of his commission, a mistake Davis later corrected.

Historians offered mixed opinions of Bragg's generalship. Stanley Horn, who chronicled the Army of Tennessee, probably called it right when he described Bragg as "a strange and unfortunate mixture." Horn credited Bragg "for the highest moral character" but in the "execution of his own plans [was] hampered by an innate vagueness of purpose."

Breckinridge, John Cabell

(1821–1875) Confederate
Senior position: Secretary of War
Final rank: Major General

Breckinridge chose politics and in 1857, at age thirty-five, became James Buchanan's vice president. In 1859, eighteen months before completing his term, the Kentucky legislature elected him to the U.S. Senate. In 1860 Democrats split and southern extremists nominated him for president. Breckinridge attempted to decline, knowing

Above: A former vice-president of the U.S., Breckinridge served the Confederacy as a general and ended up as its secretary of war.

he could not win. He opposed war but in November 1861, after Kentucky declared for the Union, he accepted a brigadier's commission in the Confederate army. Five months later President Davis promoted him to major general.

As a commander, Breckinridge saw much of the South. In April 1862 he commanded a corps at Shiloh. In August he led the attack on Baton Rouge, Louisiana. In December he fought at Stones River in Bragg's Army of Tennessee. In 1863 he served at Chickamauga and commanded a corps at Missionary Ridge. In 1864 President Davis put him in charge of southwestern Virginia where on May 15 he won a small but crucial Battle of New Market. General Lee ordered him to Richmond in time to participate in the Confederate victory at Cold Harbor, after which he served under General Early in the Shenandoah Valley until February 1865, when President Davis appointed him secretary of war. When the war ended, Breckinridge escaped to Cuba and spent three years in exile before returning home to resume the practice of law.

Brown, Isaac Newton

(1817–1889) Confederate
Senior position: Captain of the *Charleston*, CSA Navy
Final rank: Commander

Brown commanded the CSS *Arkansas* in one of history's most daring naval exploits. In July 1862, with both the Union riverine fleet and Farragut's blue-water fleet besieging Vicksburg, the *Arkansas* blasted its way out of the Yazoo River, only to encounter thirty Federal warships in the Mississippi. Firing back on every side, *Arkansas* cut a bloody swath through the fleets to arrive beneath the protective guns of Vicksburg. Assailed again by vengeful Union ships, *Arkansas* held its own, though finally had to be scuttled on its next expedition when its engines failed.

Above: Confederates are repulsed at Crawfish Creek during the Battle of Chickamauga, fought in northwestern Georgia, September 19–20, 1863.

Above: Brown made the most of what he had to work with in the Confederate Navy, especially when he commanded the *Arkansas*.

Buchanan, Franklin

(1800–1874) Confederate
Senior position: Fleet commander
Final rank: Admiral

Buckner, Simon Bolivar

(1823–1914) Confederate
Senior position: Commander, Department of East Tennessee
Final rank: Lieutenant General

A Marylander, Buchanan could not at first decide where his loyalties lay. He joined the Confederate navy in September 1861, took command of the CSS *Virginia*, and on March 9, 1862, fought the first battle between ironclads. Being a fighter rather than an administrator, Buchanan later commanded the ironclad CSS *Tennessee* during the Battle of Mobile Bay.

Above: A courageous ship commander, Buchanan (shown with an unidentified companion) always fought against the odds.

Born in Kentucky, Buckner declined a brigadier general-ship in the Union Army and in September 1861 accepted the same rank from the Confederacy. Sent to Fort Donelson, he reported to Brigadier General John Floyd as third in command. When General Grant attacked the fort on February 12, 1862, Floyd fled with Brigadier General

Above: After Fort Donelson, Buckner was able to redeem himself at further battles, particularly Chickamauga.

Gideon Pillow, who was second in command. Before the two political generals departed, they gave Buckner the dubious distinction of surrendering the fort unconditionally. Buckner spent the next six months of the war on parole.

Released to resume military operations in August 1862, Buckner joined General Bragg in Kentucky and led a division during the abortive Perryville campaign in October. Buckner's brigade suffered heavy losses breaking the Federal line, and General Hardee, commanding the division, failed to follow up the opportunity to win a victory.

While commanding the Department of East Tennessee in August 1863, Buckner received orders to join General Bragg in Georgia. He arrived with his corps just in time to participate in the Battle of Chickamauga. Shortly afterward, Buckner transferred to the Trans-Mississippi to serve as General E. Kirby Smith's chief of staff. After the war, Buckner eventually returned to Kentucky and became governor of the state in 1887 and a vice presidential nominee in 1896.

Below: The decisive bayonet charge by Grant's Iowa Second Regiment on the rebel entrenchment at Fort Donelson, February 15, 1862, forced Buckner to surrender.

Buell, Don Carlos
(1818–1898) Federal
Senior position: Commander, Army of the Cumberland
Final rank: Major General

Transferred from the Department of the Pacific in September 1861, Buell assisted General McClellan in training the Army of the Potomac before receiving command of the Army of Ohio. President Lincoln persistently prodded Buell's 50,000-man army to act. Buell eventually captured Nashville virtually unopposed. He later arrived at Shiloh in

Above: Buell was initially considered one of the best Union generals, until he failed to stop Bragg's 1862 invasion of Kentucky.

time to stem the Confederate assault and turn possible defeat into Union victory.

While serving under General Halleck at Corinth, Buell received promotion to major general and in June 1862 began advancing toward Chattanooga with four divisions. His movements were slow and sluggish because of being constantly harassed by Confederate cavalry. Instead of moving on Chattanooga, Buell evacuated Tennessee and moved back into Kentucky to impede an invasion by Confederates under General Bragg. He stopped Bragg at Perryville but failed to vigorously pursue him. Bragg moved back into Tennessee and regained control of most of the state. Severely criticized by the public for failing to pursue Bragg, coupled with habitually slow movements, Lincoln authorized Buell's removal from command on October 24, 1862. A personally courageous man but deliberately cautious, Buell spent the balance of the war "waiting orders" at Indianapolis.

Below: Buell's timely arrival saved Grant from a renewed battering at Shiloh, April 6–7, 1862.

Buford, John
(1826–1863) Federal
Senior position: Division
    commander, Army of the
    Potomac
Final rank: Major General

Returning from the frontier in October 1861, Buford entered the war in the east as a cavalry commander in General Pope's Army of Virginia. After recovering from a severe wound at Second Manassas, he reached the apogee of his career at Gettysburg. By dismounting his troopers on the first day of battle, he held off the advance of A. P. Hill's corps until reinforcements arrived.

Above: Though best known for Gettysburg, Buford had an outstanding, if short, career as a cavalry leader.

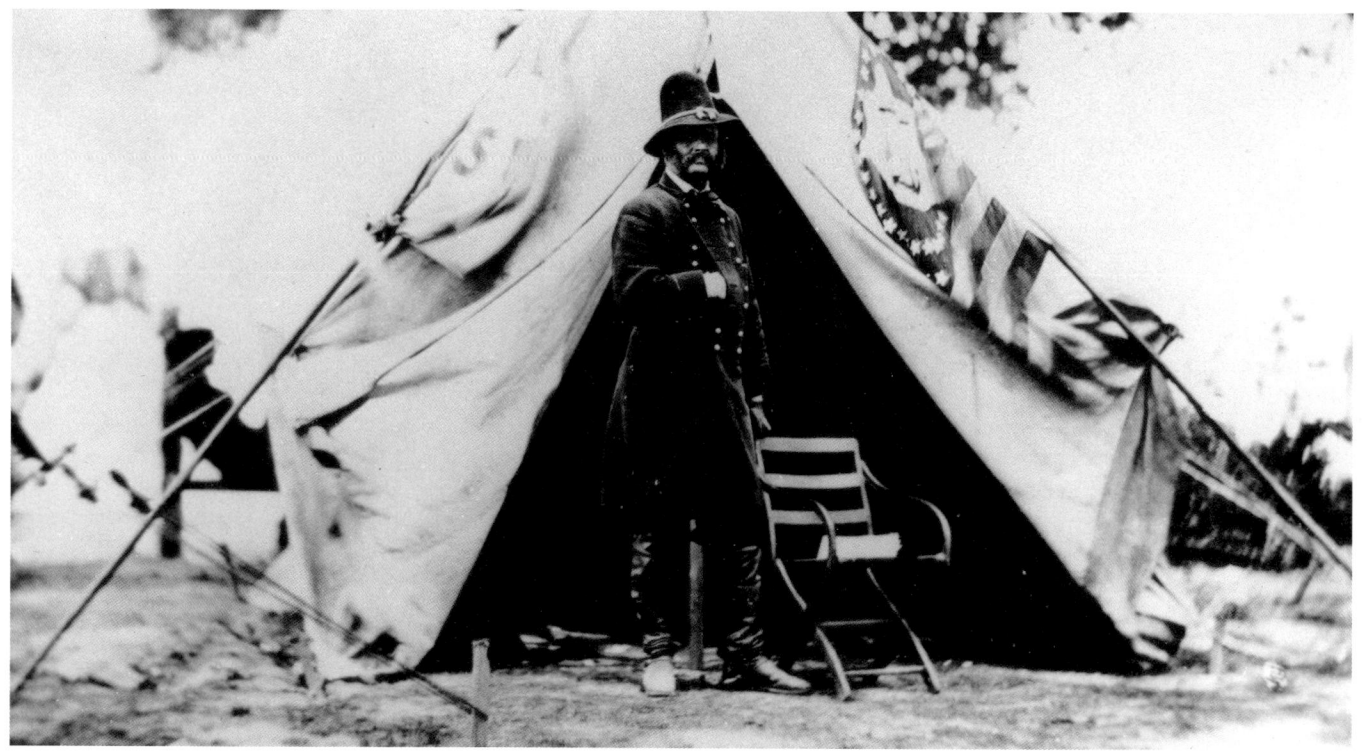

Burnside, Ambrose E.

(1824–1881) Federal
Senior position: Commander, Army
of the Potomac
Final rank: Major General

Burnside spent most of his early career on garrison duty and resigned in 1853 to manufacture a breech-loading rifle he designed while in the service. The venture failed, but Burnside remained nonchalant. He made friends easily, enjoyed playing poker, joined the state militia as a major general, and went to work for George B. McClellan on the Illinois Central. Civil War brought the two

men together again.

Burnside moved rapidly up the chain of command because he was likable, appeared to be knowledge-able, and performed well at First Manassas. He also had the good fortune in February 1862 of leading a successful coastal expedition against North Carolina, which netted several Union bases. Lincoln admired Burnside, credited him as having exceptional command capabilities, and raised him to major general.

In July 1862, after General McClellan's Peninsula campaign turned to defeat, Lincoln offered reinforcements from Burnside's command. During this period the

Above: Burnside took command of the Army of the Potomac with reluctance, which was soon verified by his lack of success.

president also became disgusted with McClellan's "slows" and offered Burnside command of the Army of the Potomac. Burnside understood his limitations and turned down the offer twice.

When General Lee invaded Maryland in September 1862, Burnside joined McClellan and assumed command of the I and IX Corps. Failing to exercise initiative during the Antietam campaign, Burnside lost the opportunity to crush weak Confederate forces holding the

opposite side of the Antietam Creek bridge. Had he moved with alacrity, his forces could have rolled up Lee's flank and inflicted severe damage. Instead, "Burnside Bridge" left the general with a black mark on his legacy and McClellan with someone to blame for not performing better at Antietam.

After McClellan failed to pursue Lee's army, Lincoln became immensely frustrated and ordered Burnside to take command of the Army of the Potomac. The order distressed Burnside to the extent that he suffered intense anxiety. Through the issuance of unclear and unsound orders at Fredericksburg, the army suffered 13,000 casualties. The losses shattered his ability to think strategically or tactically, and 1863 ended in disaster with "Burnside's Mud March," which ultimately led to his removal from command. One corps commander declared, "Burnside was fast losing his mind."

Given another chance, Burnside took command of his old IX Corps and served under Grant. His failure to move quickly after the explosion of the Crater on July 30, 1864, resulted in horrendous losses. Removed from command for the improper handing of his troops, Burnside resigned his commission on April 15, 1865.

Above left: Burnside's Union forces had to use pontoons to cross the deep Rappahannock River to attack Fredericksburg, a terrifyingly dangerous enterprise.

Left: Burnside managed to cross the creek at Antietam over a bridge that bears his name, only for his advance to be halted when the Confederate A. P. Hill hit the Federals with a devastating counterblow.

Butler, Benjamin Franklin

(1818–1893) Federal
Senior position: Commander, Army of the James
Final rank: Major General

An active criminal lawyer and powerful Democrat, Butler had developed well-honed administrative and manipulative skills but no professional military experience when President Lincoln made him a general. Butler preferred acting independently and almost drove Maryland out of the Union by an unauthorized attack on Baltimore. Lincoln tried to keep the general out of trouble by sending him to Fort Monroe, but Butler embarrassed the government by declaring emancipation for slaves he scooped up as

"contraband."

Lincoln believed Butler would be less trouble if removed from eastern operations and sent him to occupy New Orleans after David Farragut's fleet captured the city. Butler accomplished little of military value and ruled by punishing anyone who disagreed with his policies. He issued his infamous "Woman Order," a decree to stop women from insulting Federal troops, and he hanged a man

Above: Butler, postwar, with other members of Congress who oversaw impeachment proceedings during clashes over Reconstruction of the defeated South.
Left: Butler, known to Confederates as "the Beast," not only had a checkered career in military occupation but failed Grant mightily as a general.

for hauling down a Union flag. Serious problems began when he confiscated $800,000 from a Dutch consul and became known locally as "Spoons Butler" for stealing silverware from local citizens. Butler went to New Orleans with a modest net worth and died with an estate of $7 million, part of the plunder from New Orleans.

After Lincoln recalled Butler, the feisty general demonstrated his dazzling ineptitude for tactics by bottling up the Army of the James at Bermuda Hundred and later deserting forces he had put ashore at Fort Fisher. Having won reelection for a second term, Lincoln no longer needed Butler's political support and in January 1865 authorized Grant to remove the general from command.

Butterfield, Daniel

(1831–1901) Federal
Senior position: Corps commander, Army of the Potomac
Final rank: Major General

Canby, Edward R.S.

(1817–1873) Federal
Senior position: Commander, Military Division of West Mississippi
Final rank: Major General

Butterfield served with the Army of the Potomac and suffered a wound at Gaines's Mill. Some thirty years later he received the Medal of Honor for his actions there. He became a division commander after Antietam and a corps commander at Fredericksburg. While serving under Hooker as chief of staff, he designed the first corps badges for the army. His legacy, however, was composing the bugle call "Taps" in 1862 at Harrison's Landing.

Above: Butterfield was a mainstay of the Army of the Potomac, participating in many of its major battles.

Canby spent most of his fighting career in the West, where he prevented the Confederate invasion of California. After suppressing the draft riots in New York City in July 1863, he returned to western Mississippi as department commander. He supported Farragut in the capture of Mobile Bay and on April 12, 1865, accepted the surrender of the last Confederate force in the field.

Above: Canby was a true gentleman commander, only falling after the war when he was murdered by a Modoc Indian at a peace conference.

Chalmers, James R.

(1831–1898) Confederate
Senior position: Division
commander, Army of Tennessee
Final rank: Brigadier General

Chalmers began his Civil War career in the infantry and led a brigade at Shiloh. With General Bragg he fought in Kentucky and at Murfreesboro before transferring to the cavalry. He joined General Forrest as a division commander and played a brilliant role in Mississippi, Kentucky, and during Hood's 1864 campaign in Tennessee.

Above: Chalmers is best remembered as Forrest's righthand man during the last year of the war.

Chamberlain, Joshua Lawrence

(1828–1914) Federal
Senior position: Division
commander, Army of the
Potomac
Final rank: Major General

Although planning to study abroad, Chamberlain changed his mind, took leave from his professorship at Bowdoin College, and on August 8,

Below: A true "citizen soldier," Chamberlain inspired many with his bravery, fortitude, and dedication to the Union cause.

1862, joined the 20th Maine as lieutenant colonel. After very little military preparation, the war department hustled the regiment into the V Corps of the Army of the Potomac. A few weeks later Chamberlain survived his first test under fire at Antietam, the bloodiest day of the war.

When Chamberlain reached Fredericksburg in December 1862, he began to feel like a veteran. That was before Sumner sent the 20th Maine in a frontal attack against Longstreet's sharpshooters in the sunken road below Marye's Hill. Chamberlain and his men spent the freezing cold night of December 13 pinned down under relentless Confederate fire. Now well-baptized to bloody fighting, Chamberlain became involved in another poorly executed battle five months later at Chancellorsville, where he earned his eagle and full command of the 20th Maine. When General Lee slipped away from General Hooker at Chancellorsville, Chamberlain gathered together his regiment and followed the Army of the Potomac to Pennsylvania.

When the next great battle erupted across the wheat fields and peach orchards of Gettysburg, Chamberlain took position on Cemetery Hill. Suddenly, at 4:00 P.M. General Gouverneur Warren appeared on the field and ordered Strong Vincent to move his brigade to the Round Tops, which were under attack by Hood's division. The 20th Maine arrived first with 308 men and occupied the southern side of Little Round Top. Though outnumbered, Chamberlain survived the Confederate onslaught. When out of ammunition, he ordered a bayonet charge that repulsed the enemy and prevented the Confederates from rolling up the Federal flank. Thirty

Below: Thirty years after the war, Chamberlain was awarded the Medal of Honor for his courageous actions at Gettysburg, where he led a bayonet charge when his men ran out of ammunition.

Above: Chamberlain recovered from a near-mortal wound to preside over the official surrender of Lee's army at Appomattox.

years later Chamberlain received the Medal of Honor for gallantry at Gettysburg. In all, Chamberlain fought in twenty-four engagements, including Spotsylvania, Cold Harbor, Petersburg, and Five Forks. He was severely wounded during the Petersburg assaults in June 1864, and his valor so impressed Grant that he promoted Chamberlain on the field to brigadier general. To Grant's surprise, Chamberlain recovered and rejoined the army. Brevetted major general, Chamberlain fought through the final days of the war and earned the distinction of formally accepting the surrender of General Lee on April 12, 1865, at Appomattox. As a final gesture he brought his men to attention as the rabble of Lee's once vaunted army stacked their rifles and departed in peace.

Cheatham, Benjamin Franklin
(1820–1886) Confederate
Senior position: Corps commander, Army of Tennessee
Final rank: Major General

Despite being a farmer, Cheatham studied military tactics. He quickly became a gifted brigade, division, and corps commander. He fought at Belmont, Shiloh, Perryville, Stones River, Chickamauga, Missionary Ridge, Kennesaw Mountain, Atlanta, and Nashville. Cheatham eventually surrendered with Joe Johnston on April 18, 1865, in North Carolina. With no war to fight, Cheatham resumed farming.

Above: Cheatham fought like a lion for the Army of Tennessee, though many suspected he had a flask in hand, especially at Spring Hill, TN.

Cleburne, Patrick Ronayne

(1828–1864) Confederate
Senior position: Division commander, Army of
    Tennessee
Final rank: Major General

Before coming to the United States from Ireland, Cleburne served in Her Majesty's 41st Regiment of Foot, which provided his military background. He eventually settled in Helena, Arkansas, and became a successful druggist and lawyer. After his state seceded, he joined the 15th

Above: Sometimes called the "Stonewall of the West," there was no more valiant fighter for the Confederacy than the Irishman Cleburne.

Arkansas as a private. His friends immediately elected him captain and eventually colonel, which put him on track to becoming one of the Confederacy's great generals.

While serving under Major General William J. Hardee in Kentucky, Cleburne coupled his British military training and his natural charm to win the loyalty of his men and the respect of the general. Hardee rewarded Cleburne with temporary brigade command, which on March 4, 1862, became permanent.

Cleburne's first battle occurred at Shiloh, where on the morning of April 6, 1862, he led the advance on the Confederate left. After being momentarily stopped, he rallied the brigade and drove the Federals through their camps to the Tennessee River. The following day, with his force cut to 800 effectives, he staunched a Confederate rout by counterattacking and fought a rearguard action while other units retreated.

In recognition of his outstanding performance at Shiloh, Cleburne received command of a two-brigade division when Major General E. Kirby Smith advanced into Kentucky. While fighting in the van of Smith's army at Richmond, Cleburne suffered a severe wound when a bullet punctured his cheek and knock out several teeth before exiting. He could not speak and relinquished command.

Cleburne returned to duty in September 1862 in time to lead his brigades into battle at Perryville, after which he received a major general's commission to rank from December 20, 1862. He followed Bragg into Tennessee and commanded the 2nd Division of Hardee's Corps with distinction at Stones River (Murfreesboro). After fighting at Chickamauga and Chattanooga, Cleburne engaged in all the major battles of the Atlanta campaign, during which he received the thanks of Congress for courageous action at Ringgold Gap.

During Hood's invasion of Tennessee, Cleburne became enmeshed in a series of confused orders at Spring Hill, which allowed Schofield's army to narrowly escape. The next day, shot from his horse while leading the charge at the Battle of Franklin, Cleburne grabbed another mount and was killed fifty yards from the Federal line. President Davis, on hearing the news of Cleburne's death, lamented, "A vacancy was created which will never be filled."

Corcoran, William

(1827–1863) Federal
Senior position: Division commander, Army of the Potomac
Final rank: Brigadier General

Cox, Jacob D.

(1828–1900) Federal
Senior position: Commander, Department of Ohio
Final rank: Major General

Born in Ireland, Corcoran first made a name for himself when he refused to parade his New York militia unit before Britain's Prince of Wales. All was forgiven when the Civil War broke out, and Corcoran led the 69th New York at First Bull Run. He was wounded and captured by Confederate cavalry during the battle, but even in prison he continued to make headlines as the Confederates threatened to hang him in retaliation for Union threats to hang one of their seagoing privateers. Finally released, Corcoran raised a brigade-sized force of Irishmen called the "Corcoran Legion," but died before he could lead it into action, after being thrown from a horse.

Above: Though his military experience was brief, Corcoran became an icon to the Irish population of New York.

Cox entered the army on April 23, 1861, ranking as a brigadier general from May 17, 1861. He led a brigade in western Virginia under McClellan before joining Pope's Army of Virginia. At Antietam he led the IX Corps. After commanding the Department of Ohio in 1863, he joined the XXIII Corps and fought at Atlanta, Franklin, and Nashville, later rejoining General Sherman to close out the war in North Carolina.

Above: Cox fought back at the fulcrum of Hood's Tennessee invasion. He also left behind a fascinating memoir of his service.

Crook, George
(1829–1890) Federal
Senior position: Commander, Department of West Virginia
Final rank: Major General

Crittenden, Thomas L.
(1815–1893) Federal
Senior position: Corps commander, Army of the Cumberland
Final rank: Major General

Crittenden fought at Shiloh under General Buell, received promotion to major general, and became part of General Rosecrans' army. He fought at Stones River and Tullahoma before running into problems at Chickamauga. He was one of two corps commanders who, with Rosecrans, fled back to Chattanooga during Bragg's attack. Although acquitted of cowardice, Crittenden's career remained blighted.

Above: A brave fighter, Crittenden has long taken the brunt of blame for Rosecrans' faulty dispositions at Chickamauga.

A West Point graduate, Crook returned from his post in California to take command of the 36th Ohio. After serving in western Virginia, he joined the Army of the Potomac in August 1862 as a brigade commander and fought at South Mountain and Antietam.

Crook transferred to George Thomas' Army of the Cumberland in 1863 because he wanted to command a cavalry division, and took part in the Chickamauga campaign. He grew a magnificent spread of cavalryman's whiskers before returning east in 1864 to take command of the Kanawha District in western Virginia. Crook engaged in many raids and in one pitched cavalry battle completely routed Confederate General A. G. Jenkins' vaunted cavalry at Cloyd's Mountain.

Above: After battling thousands of Rebel troops in the war, Crook became even more famous afterward, when he was turned back by Sioux at the Rosebud.

In August 1864 Crook succeeded David Hunter as commander of the Department of West Virginia. He soon joined General Philip Sheridan's Army of the Shenandoah and fought at Winchester, Fishers Hill, and Cedar Creek. On October 21, 1864, he became a major general. Exactly four months later, sixty Confederate "Partisan Rangers" broke into the Revere House in Cumberland, Maryland, and carried Crook and General Benjamin Kelley off to Richmond. Exchanged in March, Crook commanded a cavalry division for the remainder of the war. He then went back to the Revere House and married Mary Daily, the proprietor's daughter.

Below: Crook was with Sheridan when he rallied his retreating troops at Cedar Creek, Shenandoah, October 19, 1864.

Curtis, Samuel Ryan
(1817–1876) Federal
Senior position: Commander, Department of Missouri
Final rank: Major General

Curtis resigned his congressional seat in August 1861 to accept an appointment as brigadier general in charge of volunteers. He commanded Federal forces at Pea Ridge (March 6–8, 1862) and earned promotion to major general. He also conducted a brilliant 1,000-mile march to Helena, Arkansas, after which he commanded the Department of Missouri.

Above: Though largely out of the public spotlight in the Trans-Mississippi, Curtis played a major role in expanding Union influence.

Custer, George Armstrong

(1839–1876) Federal
Senior position: Division commander, Army of the Potomac
Final rank: Major General

From First Manassas to Lee's surrender at Appomattox, Custer fought in every battle of the Army of the Potomac but one. Having graduated last in his class at West Point, he had something to prove. Being headstrong and contemptuous of army regulations, he made few friends and many enemies, but no one had more thirst for glory than Custer. He lost eleven horses shot from under him but suffered only one minor wound.

Having observed Custer's heroic charge during the Battle of Aldie in June 1863, General Pleasonton recommended that the fearless cavalryman be promoted from caption to brigadier general. At twenty-three, Custer became the youngest general in the Union army. He took command of the Michigan Brigade (Second Brigade, 3rd Cavalry Division) just in time to lead his men to more laurels at Gettysburg.

During Grant's spring campaign in 1864, Custer out-dueled Jeb Stuart and drove the Confederate cavalry back to Yellow Tavern, where Stuart met death. In October 1864 Custer took command of the 3rd Cavalry Division and became General Sheridan's top cavalry commander in the Shenandoah Valley. By 1865,

Above: Custer (right) sits with an old West Point friend, captured Confederate Lieutenant James B. Washington, at Fair Oaks, Virginia, May 31, 1862.

Right: Custer was called the "Boy General," having been promoted to brigade command at the age of twenty-three.

Custer, with his long golden ringlets, had become a national hero. The Confederates could not kill him no matter how often they tried, but the Sioux at Little Bighorn did.

Dahlgren, John A.B.
(1809–1870) Federal
Senior position: Commander, South Atlantic Blockading Squadron
Final rank: Rear Admiral

Davis, Jefferson C.
(1828–1879) Federal
Senior position: Corps commander, Army of the Cumberland
Final rank: Major General

Dahlgren commanded the Washington Navy Yard at the outbreak of the war and in 1862 the Bureau of Ordnance before assuming command of the South Atlantic Blockading Squadron. He is best remembered for inventing three guns—bronze boat howitzers and rifles, huge iron smoothbore "Dahlgren" shellguns, and iron rifled cannon.

Davis' war began on April 12, 1861, as a lieutenant of artillery at Fort Sumter. He rapidly progressed in rank, leading a brigade at Wilson's Creek, a division at Pea Ridge, and a corps during the Atlanta campaign. He is best remembered for an altercation with General William Nelson, his commanding officer, whom he mortally wounded after being insulted publicly in a Louisville hotel.

Above: "Dahlgren guns" became a common phrase both during the Civil War and afterward.

Above: Davis accompanied Sherman on his March to the Sea and caused a scandal when he took up a pontoon bridge before following slaves could cross.

Deas, Zachariah C.

(1819–1882) Confederate
Senior position: Brigade commander, Army of
Tennessee
Final rank: Brigadier General

Deas led the 22nd Alabama at Shiloh and suffered a severe wound. He recovered in time to join Bragg's invasion of Kentucky. Promoted to brigadier general, he led his brigade of five Alabama regiments at Stones River, Chickamauga, Chattanooga, Atlanta, Franklin, Memphis, and the Carolinas. Having seen enough war, he settled in New York City, became a cotton broker, and bought a seat on the New York stock exchange.

Above: A man who fought his heart out for the Confederacy, Deas adjusted with aplomb to the postwar era.

Deshler, James

(1833–1863) Confederate
Senior position: Brigade commander, Army of
Tennessee
Final rank: Brigadier General

Deshler never resigned from the U.S. Army: he simply joined the Confederate army as an artillery captain without giving notice. While serving in western Virginia he was shot through both thighs. Fully recovered, he became General Holmes' artillery chief in the Seven Days battles. Deshler later joined General Cleburne's division in the Army of Tennessee and was killed during the Battle of Chickamauga.

Above: Deshler had poor luck in the war, but died gallantly at the head of his troops in the Confederacy's greatest victory in the west.

Dodge, Grenville M.

(1831–1916) Federal
Senior position: Corps commander,
Army of the Tennessee
Final rank: Major General

A brilliant engineer, Dodge went to war as colonel of the 4th Iowa and moved quickly to brigade command in the Army of Southwest Missouri. After recovering from a wound at Pea Ridge, he commanded a division and then a corps in the Army of the Tennessee. Promoted to major general at Grant's request, Dodge joined Sherman in the Atlanta campaign and served gallantly until wounded in the head. After the war Dodge engineered the building of the Union Pacific Railroad, which still passes through Dodge City.

Donelson, Daniel Smith

(1801–1863) Confederate
Senior position: Brigade commander,
Army of the Tennessee
Final rank: Major General

Donelson chose the site for a Tennessee fort that carried his name. He also joined General Bragg at Tupelo to command a Tennessee brigade. During the Battle of Stones River the brigade captured 1,000 Federal troops and eleven cannon. Uninformed of Donelson's death by natural causes on April 17, 1863, the Confederate war department promoted him to major general.

Above: Dodge proved an enormous asset to Sherman, not just for his generalship but for his railroad expertise.
Right: A solid if unspectacular field commander, Donelson will always be remembered for the fort that bore his name.

Doubleday, Abner

(1819–1893) Federal
Senior position: Division commander, Army of the Potomac
Final rank: Major General

Duke, Basil W.

(1838–1916) Confederate
Senior position: Brigade commander, Army of the Tennessee
Final rank: Brigadier General

Some authorities doubt Doubleday's claim that he fired the first shot from Fort Sumter at the rebels. Doubleday relished taking credit, like the canard he had invented baseball. To the positive side, Doubleday came on the field during the first day at Gettysburg and, after General Reynolds fell, organized a creditable defense against the Confederate advance.

Above: A Union political general, Doubleday managed to become famous in more ways than one.

Brother-in-law of General John Hunt Morgan, Duke was almost hanged as a spy by both sides before joining Morgan's "Lexington Rifles." Released after being captured during Morgan's 1863 Ohio raid, Duke commanded a cavalry brigade. During the final days Duke escorted the escape of Jefferson Davis and fugitives from the Confederate government to Georgia.

Above: Morgan's right hand, Duke was the epitome of the dashing Rebel cavalryman that Sherman, for one, most feared.

Early, Jubal A.

(1816–1894) Confederate
Senior position: Corps commander,
Army of Northern Virginia
Final rank: Lieutenant General

Early's men called him "Old Jube" and accepted him as a sharp-tongued, hard-drinking leader who fought with determination but not always wisely. He voted against secession in 1861 but went to war because he enjoyed good, hard fighting. His superiors were so impressed with Early's performance at First Manassas that they made him a brigadier general in the Army of Northern Virginia.

Early took a bullet in the shoulder while defending the Peninsula in May 1862 against the invasion of the Army of the Potomac. He remained on the field until forcibly taken to a hospital in Williamsburg. Impatient for action, he took command of one of Stonewall Jackson's brigades in time for the Battle of Malvern Hill, but got lost and never fired a shot.

Early's next escapade occurred at Cedar Mountain, where he held back Banks' corps but suffered heavy casualties. With skillful maneuvering, he deceived General John Pope's Army of Virginia at Warrenton Springs and set up General Lee's victory at Second Manassas. A month later at Antietam he fought his brigade courageously with little loss.

Lee awarded Early's brilliant performance at Fredericksburg with command of a division and promotion to major general. One of Early's

weaknesses became manifest at Chancellorsville when he failed to reconnoiter. Lee, however, had

Above: "Old Jube" had a contentious career, both during the war and afterward—but he was always a fighter.

49

admired Early's pugnacity and in May 1864 raised him to lieutenant general.

After Cold Harbor, Lee detached Early's II Corps and sent it to the Shenandoah Valley to create a disturbance. Early caused more than a disturbance. He notched a decisive victory in Maryland at Monocacy, raided the outskirts of Washington and threatened the capital, burned Chambersburg, Pennsylvania, in reprisal for destruction in the

Shenandoah Valley, and retired to Winchester with his troops shoeless and exhausted.

Early's men got little rest. Major General Philip Sheridan outgeneraled Old Jube in the valley, striking first at Winchester, then at Fishers Hill and Cedar Creek. By October, Early's corps had been whittled to shreds. Those who survived the Federal onslaught finally surrendered to General Custer at Waynesboro,

Above: Jubal Early's command was effectively ended at the Battle of Cedar Creek, which resulted in a crushing defeat for the Confederacy.

Virginia, in March 1865. Deeply troubled by the depredations of his recent campaign, Early sought refuge in Mexico and later in Canada. He eventually returned to Lynchburg, Virginia, and resumed the practice of law.

Ellet, Alfred W.

(1820–1895) Federal
Senior position: Commander, Mississippi Marine Brigade
Final rank: Brigadier General

Ewell, Richard Stoddert

(1817–1872) Confederate
Senior position: Corps commander, Army of Northern Virginia
Final rank: Lieutenant General

Ellet commanded one of the strangest units in the Union. With his brother Charles, he created a flotilla of rams for the war department, destroyed the Confederate River Defense Fleet, and captured Memphis. He then organized the Mississippi Marine Brigade and used the same vessels to raid Confederate towns and plantations. He sometimes assisted Grant, but mostly caused trouble for everyone.

Above: Ellet, a creative individual, caused havoc with his strange Mississippi "Ram Fleet."

A grumpy Indian fighter known as "Old Bald Head," Ewell commanded the Second Brigade at First Manassas. Raised to major general in January 1862, he joined General Jackson in the Shenandoah Valley and commanded a division at Winchester and Cross Keys. He complained regularly because Jackson never gave him orders until the last minute.

Above: Ewell replaced Stonewall Jackson as head of the Army of Northern Virginia's Second Corps.

Ewell remained with Jackson through the Seven Days battles, Cedar Mountain, and Second Manassas, where he lost a leg a Groveton. While recuperating, and having been a confirmed bachelor, Ewell nevertheless married a woman he introduced to everyone as "the Widow Brown." Equipped with a wooden leg, he had to be helped onto his horse, so usually rode in an ambulance.

Injury and marriage took some of the fight out of Ewell, and two more wounds only added to his miseries. He commanded the II Corps from Gettysburg to Spotsylvania, but without the tactical instincts of Jackson. He fell from his horse at Bloody Angle, which left him temporarily incapacitated. Ewell held minor posts for the balance of the war and for a while commanded the defenses of Richmond. He abandoned the capital on Lee's orders and fell into the hands of the Federals at Sayler's Creek on April 6, 1865.

Below: The Battle of Spotsylvania, Virginia. At one point, Ewell became hysterical, beating some of his fleeing soldiers with his sword until Lee restrained him.

Farnsworth, Elon John
(1837–1863) Federal
Senior position: Brigade commander, Army of the Potomac
Final rank: Major General

Farnsworth joined his father's regiment (8th Illinois Cavalry) on September 18, 1861, and is said to have never missed a battle or skirmish during the rest of his career. During the Battle of Gettysburg, General Kilpatrick ordered him to charge Confederate infantry and artillery protected on high ground behind stone walls. Farnsworth protested but followed orders, and after losing much of his command, died with his men.

Above: Elevated along with Custer as a "boy general" just prior to Gettysburg, Farnsworth died gallantly while obeying misguided orders.

Farragut, David Glasgow

(1801–1870) Federal
Senior position: Commander, West Gulf Blockading Squadron
Final rank: Admiral

Farragut had been in the navy fifty-one years when the Civil War began. Despite being from Tennessee and living in Virginia, he remained loyal to the Union. He never received much in the way of an education. The sea had been his life.

In December 1861 Secretary of the Navy Gideon Welles gave him command of the West Gulf Blockading Squadron, provided him with a squadron of deep-draft ocean-going warships, and directed him to enter the Mississippi River and capture New Orleans, the South's largest and wealthiest city. Some thought the task impossible. Farragut spent nearly a month getting his ships over the Mississippi bar and into the river. When ascending the river, he found chains stretched across the Mississippi below two of the strongest forts in the Confederacy. Any ship passing between Fort Jackson and Fort St. Philip invited heavy crossfire. In the early morning hours of April 24, 1862, Farragut's seventeen steam sloops and gunboats ran the gauntlet between the forts, destroyed the waiting Confederate squadron, and

Right: An aggressive commander, Farragut established himself as one of the great naval leaders in history during the Civil War.

on the following day captured New Orleans. Overnight, Farragut became a national hero. He received the thanks of Congress and on July 16 became the navy's first rear admiral.

Instead of returning to the gulf where his ships belonged, Farragut passed Port Hudson to help Grant capture Vicksburg. Finding Grant north of Vicksburg, Farragut patrolled the river and blockaded Port Hudson. He eventually turned the river over to David Porter and took many of his ships back to sea.

After a short leave in New York City, Farragut returned to the gulf in 1864 intent on capturing Mobile Bay. Two forts stood watch over the entrance channel, which was also seeded with torpedoes (technically, submerged mines). The *Tennessee*, the most powerful ironclad built by the Confederacy, lay inside the bay with several gunboats. On the morning of August 5 Farragut advanced, watching as a torpedo sank the monitor USS *Tecumseh*. When the lead

Left: In the Battle of Mobile Bay Farragut hangs from the tops as his flagship exchanges broadsides with the Rebel ironclad *Tennessee*.
Below: Having beaten the *Tennessee* into submission, Farragut repaired the ironclad and used her a few days later to force the surrender of Fort Morgan.

ship stopped, Farragut leaned from a yardarm and hollered, "Damn the torpedoes! Full speed ahead!" By 11:00 A.M., Confederate naval resistance ended. The Battle of Mobile Bay became Farragut's greatest victory. Once again thanked by Congress, he became the navy's first vice admiral, and after the war, the government promoted him to full admiral.

Foote, Andrew Hull

(1806–1863) Federal
Senior position: Commander, South Atlantic Blockade
** Squadron**
Final rank: Rear Admiral

Forrest, Nathan Bedford

(1821–1877) Confederate
Senior position: Commander, Forrest's Cavalry
** Department**
Final rank: Lieutenant General

Given command of the western flotilla at the beginning of the war, Foote assembled a squadron of river gunboats and in February 1862 aided Grant in the capture of Fort Henry and Fort Donelson. Although wounded at Donelson, he aided General Pope in capturing the upper Mississippi. Promoted to rear admiral, he returned east to command the South Atlantic Blockading Squadron. Because of the unhealed wound, he died on the way to his new command.

Above: Foote's riverine fleet helped mightily in achieving Grant's first victories in the west.

"The most remarkable man our Civil War produced on either side," was William Tecumseh Sherman's postwar comment on Forrest, though during the conflict itself Sherman had called him "the very devil."

Forrest not only lacked West Point training, he had hardly any education at all, and was nearly forty when he enlisted as a private in the Confederate service. Yet he did have some leadership experience: first by raising a pack of brothers after his father died (he had also lost his twin sister, Fanny); and second through becoming a millionaire

Above: Forrest became legendary in his time as the "Wizard of the Saddle," and his reputation has grown since.

the advent of panzer divisions.

His first notoriety came at Fort Donelson when, after pitching into the battle for the fort, he refused to surrender his command and escaped with a thousand men across an icy stream. After supervising the evacuation of stores from Nashville, he fought at Shiloh, and repulsed the Federal pursuit after the Confederate army had been forced to retreat.

While leading 1,200 cavalrymen in advance of Bragg's invasion of Kentucky, Forrest captured a similar number of Union troops at Murfreesboro by attacking each regiment in turn. It was while describing this fight that he supposedly uttered his famous philosophy of warfare: "Get there first with the most men." (Or, as it was derided by Northerners, "Git thar fustest with the mostest.") It was not a reference to superior forces, which he almost never had, but to the principle of maneuver that allowed him to concentrate his own strength against decisive points.

In the fall of 1862 he was stripped of his command and ordered to assemble a new one, whereupon he was launched against Grant's supply lines in western Tennessee. This he accomplished so well that Grant was forced to abandon his first drive on Vicksburg, and the railroad in that area was rendered unusable for the rest of the war.

In late winter and into the spring of 1863 Forrest wreaked havoc on Union outposts and columns, "fighting by ear," as he called it, while "keeping the skeer on 'em." That spring he chased down a major Union raiding force led by Abel Streight, bringing it to heel just short of Rome, Georgia. Using artifice to exaggerate his numbers, some 1,600 Federals surrendered to Forrest's command of about 500 weary troops.

At the Battle of Chickamauga, Forrest fought on the Confederate

businessman, primarily through the practice of slave trading. He may not have been able to properly read when the war began, but he did know something about supply, logistics, and command.

Forrest did not stay a private for long, as the governor of Tennessee asked him to raise a regiment of "mounted rangers." Thus was born Forrest's Cavalry, which went on to rewrite the rulebook on mounted warfare and, as some say, presaged

Above: The most famous picture of Forrest, with hair slicked back, which was not usual for him in the field.

Right: Forrest's surprise raid on Memphis in August 1864, when he circled a Federal army to re-enter his old hometown.

Left: The statue of Forrest over his grave in Memphis, which still stands, despite many civic arguments to take it down.

Transferred west per his own wishes, Forrest went on to his greatest exploits, alternating invasions of western Tennessee with repelling Union counter-incursions into northern Mississippi. Notable among these battles was Fort Pillow, where Forrest's command was accused of slaughtering U.S. Colored Troops who had surrendered, and Brice's Crossroads, where with 3,200 cavalry he utterly demolished a Union force of over 8,000.

This area of operations became increasingly crucial in the summer of 1864, as Sherman's drive on Atlanta got underway and one of his main imperatives was to keep Forrest off his supply lines. "There will never be peace in Tennessee until Forrest is dead," said the Union general, as he launched repeated assaults into northern Mississippi to tie Forrest down. When the largest of these—some 18,000 men under A. J. Smith—approached, Forrest simply went around it and raided the city of Memphis.

When finally unleashed on Sherman's supply lines, Forrest obliterated a series of Union garrisons and depots, and at one point captured several ships to create his own "navy." At the end of 1864, he rejoined the Army of Tennessee, now under Hood, and spearheaded its drive north that culminated in the battles of Franklin and Nashville. Afterward, Forrest commanded the rearguard and held off Federal pursuit. Promoted to lieutenant general (the only man in the war to rise to that rank from private), Forrest tried but failed to hold back a Federal cavalry corps four times his size at Selma. This was his last battle, albeit one in which he personally killed his thirtieth Federal soldier, a point in which he took pride, since to that date he had only lost twenty-nine horses.

After the war, Forrest was said to have helped found the original Ku Klux Klan and was named its first Grand Wizard (after his wartime nickname, "The Wizard of the Saddle"). One of the most controversial Civil War commanders, Forrest was commemorated with a huge statue that still stands in Memphis, viewed by some as a symbol of the worst of the old South, and by others as representing its martial best.

right, employing most of his men as infantry, while also using artillery to try to fend off Granger's reinforcements. After the victory he urged immediate pursuit of the disorganized Federals but Bragg did not agree. "What does he fight battles for?" was the cavalry leader's comment as he stalked out of Bragg's tent.

Frémont, John Charles

(1813–1880) Federal
Senior position: Commander, Western Department
Final ranks: Major General

Earning himself the sobriquet "The Pathfinder" for his 1840s expeditions in the west (Oregon Trail, Oregon Territory, Great Basin, and California), John Charles

Above: The Battle of Wilson's Creek, during which the egotistical Frémont suffered defeat.
Right: Frémont failed to live up to his earlier reputation at the start of the Civil War.

Frémont had also served in the Mexican-American War. So the war department expected superb performance from him when they sent him to St. Louis in charge of the Western Department. But Frémont was unjustifiably egotistical and pompous, surrounding himself with a staff that many thought more akin to a palace guard in their highhandedness and finery. He spent lavishly on forti-fying the city and his headquarters but ignored requisitioning arms and equipment for his men. He estab-lished martial law in Missouri without permission and then issued an unauthorized policy on emancipation that Lincoln irritably forced him to revoke. Frémont sent his wife to Washington to speak in his defense, but Jessie Benton Frémont only made matters worse. Her husband then suffered defeat at Wilson's Creek, but he blamed the loss on his subordi-nate, General Lyon. Lincoln eventu-ally ran out of patience with Frémont's misconduct and recalled him from St. Louis.

Instead of eliminating the problem, Lincoln put Frémont in charge of the Mountain Department. During Stonewall Jackson's Shenandoah Valley campaign, Frémont demonstrated his military ineptitude at Cross Keys on June 8, 1862, and got thoroughly whipped. When the war department transferred the corps to the Army of Virginia, Frémont refused to serve under General Pope. Relieved from duty on June 28, 1862, Frémont spent the rest of the war in New York waiting orders.

French, Samuel G.

(1818–1910) Confederate
Senior position: Division
   commander, Army of Tennessee
Final rank: Major General

French saw little fighting until he came east and commanded the rear guard on the Peninsula, which held McClellan's army in check while General Lee won the battle of Second Manassas. French wanted action, so Lee sent him to the Army of Tennessee to command a division. He fought during the Atlanta campaign and later served under Hood at Franklin and Nashville.

Above: French fought well, but had the misfortune of seeing most of his action during failed campaigns in the west.

Garfield, James A.

(1831–1881) Federal
Senior position: Chief of Staff, Army
of the Tennessee
Final rank: Major General

Garfield grew up in poverty on the frontier of Ohio and worked industriously to get an education. He became involved in politics and agreed with Lincoln's policy toward the South. On August 21, 1861, he joined the 42nd Ohio and trained recruits by reading military manuals and moving blocks around on a table. The process also taught him something about military tactics. Three months later Garfield became the regiment's colonel.

Promoted to brigadier general in January 1862, Garfield commanded a brigade in the Army of the Ohio, won a series of minor battles, and became known as the "Hero of Sandy Valley." Then came Shiloh, where Garfield began to understand the meaning of slaughter. Late in 1862 he became ill and temporarily performed court-martial duty. When he returned to the army General Rosecrans offered him the choice of brigade command or chief of staff to the Army of the Cumberland. Garfield preferred using his organizational abilities and chose the latter. While serving under Rosecrans, Garfield's home district elected him to Congress. He resigned from the army and spent the rest of his life in politics. Elected president in 1880, he was mortally wounded by a disappointed office seeker and died on September 19, 1881.

Above: A future U.S. president, Garfield compiled an excellent record in the Civil War.

Garnett, Richard Brooke

(1817–1863) Confederate
Senior position: Brigade commander, Army of Northern
  Virginia
Final rank: Brigadier General

Gillmore, Quincy Adams

(1825–1888) Federal
Senior position: Corps commander, Army of the James
Final rank: Major General

Garnett served under Jackson and eventually succeeded to the command of the famous Stonewall Brigade. Jackson arrested Garnett for withdrawing the brigade at Kernstown but dropped the charges during the Cedar Mountain campaign. Garnett grieved at Jackson's death, cleared his tarnished reputation at Gettysburg, and fell at Cemetery Hill during Pickett's Charge.

Above: Once shunned by Stonewall Jackson, Garnett died a hero's death during Pickett's Charge at Gettysburg.

During the spring of 1864 Gillmore had the misfortune of serving in General Butler's Army of the James. When Grant struck Lee that spring, the way lay open for Butler to capture Richmond. Butler bungled the opportunity. He blamed his ineptitude on Gillmore and sent him to Washington in disgrace. Gillmore redeemed himself— Butler never did.

Above: Regardless of his achievements, Gillmore may have sported the most formidable epaulettes of the war.

Gist, States Rights

(1831–1864) Confederate
Senior position: Division commander, Army of
Tennessee
Final rank: Brigadier General

Gordon, John Brown

(1832–1904) Confederate
Senior position: Corps commander, Army of Northern
Virginia
Final rank: Major General

Gist assumed command of General Bee's brigade after the latter was killed at First Manassas. He served under General Pemberton at Vicksburg and commanded General William Walker's division at Chickamauga and Missionary Ridge. During the Battle of Franklin, Gist lost his life leading his brigade into battle on foot after his horse had been shot.

Above: With one of the more curious names to emerge from the war, Gist was lost along with six other Rebel generals at Franklin.

Named colonel of the 6th Alabama, Gordon demonstrated a penchant for fighting during the Peninsula campaign and rose rapidly in the ranks, assuming temporary command of Robert Rodes' brigade during Seven Pines. While leading his regiment at Antietam, he suffered a serious head wound and almost drowned in his own blood. While recovering, Gordon received promotion to brigadier general.

Above: A brilliant commander who rose to prominence late in the conflict, Gordon also left behind a fascinating memoir.

During the Wilderness campaign Gordon began compiling a brilliant record, which during the subsequent battles soon attracted the notice of General Lee. Promoted to major general on May 14, 1864, Gordon rapidly became one of Lee's most trusted and competent field officers. During the siege of Petersburg, Lee detached Gordon's division for General Early's campaign in the Shenandoah Valley and Maryland but brought him back to command a corps during the last months of the war.

During the final days, Gordon planned and led a vicious assault on Fort Stedman, although, after plunging a huge gap in the Federal line below Petersburg, he ran out of momentum. On Lee's orders, Gordon pulled the remnants of his corps out of the Petersburg trenches on April 2, fought a running retreat across central Virginia, and surrendered his men at Appomattox.

Below: In the Battle of Antietam, Gordon led from the front, but sustained several injuries: two balls into one leg, another through his left arm, a fourth through the shoulder, and a near-fatal one in the face.

Gracie, Archibald, Jr.

(1832–1864) Confederate
Senior position: Brigade commander, Army of the
    Tennessee
Final rank: Brigadier General

Gracie led three different Alabama regiments and served under Kirby Smith in eastern Tennessee before being promoted to brigadier general in November 1862. He commanded his brigade under General Preston at Chickamauga and went with him to Virginia. After surviving the spring campaign of 1864, Gracie was cut down by a sharpshooter at Petersburg.

Above: Gracie fought everywhere he could during the war, and his brigade comprised the Rebel apex at Chickamauga.

Granbury, Hiram B.

(1831–1864) Confederate
Senior position: Brigade commander, Army of the Tennessee
Final rank: Brigadier General

Granger, Gordon

(1822–1876) Federal
Senior position: Corps commander, Army of the Cumberland
Final rank: Major General

Exchanged after the capture of Fort Donelson, Granbury (sometimes spelled "Granberry") and his 7th Texas fought in Gregg's brigade until Vicksburg fell. After Chickamauga and Missionary Ridge, he took command of James A. Smith's Texas brigade and participated in the Atlanta campaign. Following Hood's army into Tennessee, Granbury lost his life in a charge at Franklin.

Above: Gracie fought everywhere he could during the war, and his brigade comprised the Rebel apex at Chickamauga.

Granger served exclusively in the West and fought in many of the important campaigns. In the Army of Mississippi he commanded a cavalry regiment and later the 5th Infantry Division. He led a corps at Chickamauga and Missionary Ridge and later aided Admiral Farragut in the capture of Mobile Bay. Short, fiery, and profane, Granger did not inspire his troops.

Above: Granger came to George Thomas's aid just in the nick of time at Chickamauga, but had difficulty maintaining his brief renown.

Grant, Ulysses Simpson

(1822-1885) Federal

Senior position: General in Chief of the Armies of the United States

Final rank: Lieutenant General

Grant grew up in Point Pleasant, Ohio, as Hiram Ulysses, his baptized name. His name became Ulysses Simpson when the congressman who authorized Grant's appointment to West Point mistakenly dropped Hiram and accidentally wrote the maiden name of Grant's mother on the document. Thereafter, Grant became Ulysses Simpson. When he graduated from the academy in 1843—twenty-first in a class of thirty-nine—Grant excelled in horsemanship. There were no openings in the cavalry, so he joined the infantry.

During the Mexican War, Grant served in the 4th Infantry under Zachary Taylor and Winfield Scott, both of whom he admired. He took part in battles at Monterey, Molino del Rey, and Chapultepec, which earned him brevets of first lieutenant and caption. After the war he became bored in remote garrisons, drank heavily because he missed his wife and two children, and resigned to be with his family in St. Louis. Tied to living a hardscrabble existence, he was saved by the Civil War.

Appointed colonel of the 21st Illinois, Grant applied for a better military position but nobody wanted him. Ordered to Missouri, he received promotion to brigadier general through the efforts of Elihu Washburne, an Illinois congressman whose committee had four brigadierships to grant. His first command effort ended in near-disaster at Belmont. His luck changed in February 1862 when he broke the center of the Confederate defensive perimeter and captured Forts Henry and Donelson. Because of his surrender demands, U.S. Grant became known as "Unconditional Surrender" Grant.

Glory never lasts. On April 6 Confederates assaulted his scattered army at Shiloh and sent parts of it reeling back to the edge of the Tennessee River. Grant brought up reinforcements and on the following day repulsed the enemy. General Henry Halleck did not like Grant. He accused him of being drunk, criticized him for not following up the victory, and arrived from St. Louis to take charge. Halleck proved even more inert at engaging the enemy. Lincoln ordered him to Washington as

Below: Despite an unspectacular early career, Grant was given overall command of the Union's armies in March 1864.

Right: Casual and modest by nature, Grant nevertheless proved himself to be one of the most hardheaded and determined leaders of the war.

commander-in-chief, leaving Grant in command.

Grant's career began to take shape in 1863. He spent the winter keeping his force busy with efforts to flank Vicksburg. With help from Admiral Porter, he transported his army across the Mississippi River below Vicksburg on April 30 and on May 22 laid siege to the city. On July 4 Vicksburg's commander, General Pemberton, surrendered 20,000 troops. Overnight, Grant became Lincoln's man. When asked why, the president replied, "He fights."

In September, General Rosecrans came under siege at Chattanooga. When he did nothing to open his lines of communication, Lincoln sent Grant. On October 23 Grant arrived, assessed the situation, defeated General Bragg's army on Missionary Ridge and Lookout Mountain, and in late November drove the Confederates back to Chickamauga.

Lincoln had been searching for a general since the beginning of the war and now he had one. He brought Grant to Washington in March 1864, empowered him with a third star, and

Above: Grant (at left) relaxing near the summit of Lookout Mountain after his army had cleared the Rebels from the vicinity of Chattanooga.
Right: A better general than administrator, Grant was helped in writing his postwar memoir by Mark Twain.

named him general in chief with Halleck as chief of staff. Grant hated Washington and wanted to get away as quickly as possible. Lincoln agreed as long as Grant made his headquarters with the Army of the Potomac and remained in close communication.

Lincoln expected Grant to remove General Meade, but Grant liked Meade and retained him as commander of the Army of the Potomac. During the spring campaign of 1864, Grant orchestrated the army's movements and Meade conducted them. The enormously heavy casualties of the Wilderness, Spotsylvania, and Cold Harbor were all Grant's influence. He vowed not to turn back and never did. Nor did his close friend, General Sherman, who launched the Atlanta campaign. Because of horrendously inept performance by General Butler's Army of the James, Lee stopped Grant at the Petersburg trenches, and the war Grant hoped to win in 1864 dribbled into another year.

By the spring of 1865 attrition and starvation had taken a toll on Lee's army. Instead of bludgeoning Lee's forces out of the trenches with frontal attacks, Grant used finesse, speed, and tactics to empty Petersburg fortifications and drive the Army of Northern Virginia into the open. In a pursuit through central Virginia, Sheridan's cavalry blocked Lee's army at Appomattox Court House. On April 9 Grant accepted Lee's surrender graciously and paroled the vanquished. Nine days later Joe Johnston surrendered to General Sherman in North Carolina, and but for a few renegade units in the Deep South, the Civil War ended.

After the war, Grant became a full general and in 1869 the president of the United States. At heart, Grant was a warrior, and some warriors never made very good presidents.

Green, Thomas

(1814–1864) Confederate
Senior position: Brigade commander, Trans-Mississippi
Department
Final rank: Brigadier General

A Tennessee lawyer, Green enlisted to help the "Texians" win their independence from Mexico; he fought the Comanche; and then fought in the Mexican-American War. When Texas seceded, he led cavalry with distinction from New Mexico to Mississippi. Green was killed in action while leading his men against Federal gunboats patrolling the Red River in 1864.

Above: A legendary Texas fighter, Green's loss was severely felt by the Confederates in the Trans-Mississippi theater.

Grierson, Benjamin

(1826–1911) Federal
Senior position: Division commander, Army of the
Tennessee
Final rank: Major General

A prewar music teacher, Grierson became a cavalry commander and electrified the North with a raid behind Confederate lines in the spring of 1863. Starting with 1,700 men from the Tennessee border, he rode 800 miles through the state of Mississippi, finally emerging at Baton Rouge, Louisiana. Grierson's raid went far toward distracting the Confederates as Grant began his final move on Vicksburg, and proved that Federal horsemen—in the west as well as the east—had achieved near-parity with their Rebel counterparts.

Above: Grierson (at center, with hand to his chin) became famous in the North in 1863, but was afterwards repeatedly bested by Forrest.

Halleck, Henry Wager

(1815–1872) Federal
Senior position: Chief of Staff of the
U.S. Army
Final rank: Lieutenant General

Henry Halleck died at his desk in Louisville, Kentucky, administering the reconstruction of the former Confederate States of America. Had he known this in advance it would perhaps have pleased the man Abraham Lincoln referred to as "little more than a first rate clerk."

A professional soldier, Halleck's strengths were organization and planning. He was no field commander, no leader of men. Most men, in fact, considered "Old Brains"—his well-deserved nickname—to be cold, calculating and suspicious.

During the Mexican-American War, Halleck was assigned duty in California and served admirably as an aide and chief-of-staff. He helped draft the state constitution and then left the army to make his fortune as a lawyer, developer, and land speculator.

When the Civil War began, Winfield Scott brought Halleck back into service as a major general to command the western theater. There, his fortunes were bolstered by Grant's victories at Forts Henry and Donelson. After the bloody battle of Shiloh, however, Halleck did all in his power to diminish Grant's growing fame as a commander.

Lincoln brought Halleck to Washington, but found him to be a better adviser than leader, and he eventually placed Grant in command of all armies in the field. Together, the superb administrator and the dogged warrior were an unbeatable combination.

Above: "Old Brains" was less than dynamic as a field commander, but served well in Washington, where he continued as a mentor to men like Grant and Sherman.

Hampton, Wade

(1818–1902) Confederate
Senior position: Commander,
  Cavalry Corps, Army of Northern
  Virginia
Final rank: Lieutenant General

Left: A wealthy plantation owner, Hampton succeeded the legendary Stuart admirably as Lee's top cavalry commander in the east.
Above: In late summer 1864, Wade Hampton carried out an audacious raid to relieve the Union of valuable forage for its horses, in addition to thousands of beeves near Coggin's Point, south of Richmond.

Wade Hampton took command of Robert E. Lee's cavalry when Jeb Stuart was killed in 1864. From that moment, he never lost a battle. Born into South Carolina's plantation and slave owning culture, he was an audacious warrior who led his men from the front: "Charge them, my brave boys, charge them!" he shouted at Trevilian Station, Virginia, as he spurred his horse toward the dismounted Federal troopers.

Hampton's leadership was evident at war's outbreak when, spending a private fortune, he raised and outfitted six companies of infantry, four companies of cavalry, and one battery of artillery. They were "Hampton's Legion," and from the First Battle of Bull Run in 1861 where he deployed at a decisive moment, giving Stonewall Jackson's brigade time to reach the field, until the end of the war, he received five serious wounds from rifle shots and saber cuts. Hampton surrendered with Joe Johnston's army in North Carolina two weeks after Appomattox.

Angered that black Federal troops were stationed in his state during Reconstruction, Hampton championed the "Lost Cause," rationalizing the Southern defeat. He eventually served South Carolina as governor and senator. When, as an elder statesman, his stately home burned down and he was left virtually penniless, hundreds of friends and admirers contributed to build a new one.

Hancock, Winfield Scott

(1824–1886) Federal
Senior position: Corps commander, Army of the Potomac
Final rank: Major General

After graduating from West Point in 1844, Hancock earned a brevet serving in the Mexican War before being assigned to the frontier. After the outbreak of the Civil War, he became a brigadier general on September 23, 1861, and took command of the Third Brigade in William F. "Baldy" Smith's division.

Hancock served in the Army of the Potomac throughout the war. He distinguished himself during the Peninsula campaign and throughout the battles of the Seven Days. From August 1862, until January 1863 he led the 1st Division, II Corps, at Antietam, and on November 29, 1862, he received promotion to major general and at Fredericksburg assumed full command of the II Corps.

After Chancellorsville, Hancock fought the three-day battle at Gettysburg. When he arrived on the field on July 1 he found John F. Reynolds dead and Oliver H. Howard contending for command. He brushed aside Howard's grumbles, took command, and anchored the Union forces on Cemetery Hill, thereby forcing the Confederates to settle for a

Left: Hancock is often considered the best Union general who never led an army.

Above: Hancock (seated) with (left to right) Francis Barlow, John Gibbon, and David B. Barney.

less defensible ridge. On the second day, he commanded the left wing of the army and prevented General Longstreet from putting Confederate forces on the Round Tops. On the third day, while repulsing Pickett's Charge, Hancock suffered a wound from which he never fully recovered.

Still unhealed, Hancock returned to duty at the end of the year, resumed command of the II Corps, and fought in the bloody battles of the Wilderness, Spotsylvania (where his troops assaulted the "Bloody Angle"), Cold Harbor, Deep Bottom, Reams' Station, Boydton Plank Road, and Petersburg. When his wound reopened in November 1864, he refused to take leave and went to Washington to recruit a "Veterans Reserve Corps."

Hancock avoided all the carping in the Army of the Potomac and remained what General Grant called his "most conspicuous" commander. Theodore Lyman, who wrote *Meade's*

Headquarters, referred to Hancock as a man of "massive features [with] folds around the eye that often mark the man of ability." He also noted that Hancock "always has a clean *white* shirt (where he gets them nobody knows)."

Hardee, William J.
(1815–1873) Confederate
Senior position: Commander, Dept. of South Carolina, Georgia and Florida
Final rank: Lieutenant General

A West Point graduate from the class of 1838, Hardee received two brevets in the Mexican War and later returned to the academy as commandant of cadets and instructor in infantry, artillery, and cavalry tactics. During the 1850s he wrote the classic, *Rifle and Light Infantry Tactics*, best known as *Hardee's Tactics*. He resigned from the U.S. Army on January 19, 1861—twelve days after his home state of Georgia seceded—and on June 17 accepted a brigadier general's commission in the Confederate army.

Hardee organized an Arkansas brigade, which he commanded in that state until being ordered to Kentucky during the autumn of 1861. Promoted major general on October 7, 1861, Hardee joined General Albert S. Johnston just before the battle of Shiloh. Johnston put Hardee in command of the III Corps, later redesignated the I Corps but better known as Hardee's Corps.

Hardee performed creditably during the Shiloh engagement and later commanded a wing of the Army

Right: Hardee was a major figure in the US Army and the CS Army of Tennessee, the latter of which he should well have commanded.

of the Tennessee during General Bragg's Kentucky campaign. Heavily engaged at Stones River (Murfreesboro), Hardee's troops demonstrated the tactical skills taught them by their commander. His men affectionately called him "Old Reliable."

Hardee showed little respect for Bragg's leadership ability, and after the Tullahoma campaign received a transfer to Mississippi. He soon returned to the Army of the Tennessee, only to witness the collapse of most of the army in the disaster at Chattanooga. When Bragg resigned, Hardee expressed great relief.

After General Joseph Johnston took command, Hardee served during the Atlanta campaign. When offered an opportunity join John Bell Hood, Hardee considered him tactically reckless and requested a transfer. The war department responded by placing Hardee in charge of the Department of South Carolina, Florida and Georgia, which put him right in the middle of Sherman's march, which he was powerless to stop. Compelled to evacuate Savannah on December 18, 1864, Hardee eventually rejoined Joe Johnston. During the last large battle of the campaign, at

Above: Hardee tragically lost his sole son, a sixteen-year-old, at one of the war's last battles, at Bentonville.
Left: The capture of DeGress's Battery by the Confederates of Hardee's Corps at the Battle of Atlanta.

Bentonville, his only son, a teenager, died in a cavalry charge. On April 26, 1865 Hardee surrendered at Greensboro, North Carolina, and like many of the men who had fought beside him, went home and became a planter.

Hatch, Edward

(1832–1889) Federal
Senior position: Division commander, Army of the Tennessee
Final rank: Major General

Heintzelman, Samuel P.

(1805–1880) Federal
Senior position: Corps commander, Army of the Potomac
Final rank: Major General

Having volunteered for service as a private, Hatch made his fortune with calculated daring and loyalty to U.S. Grant. He led troops successfully throughout the western theater of operations—Island No. 10, the Battle of Corinth, Grierson's Raid, and during the Franklin and Nashville campaign. After the war, he remained in the army and served in the U.S. southwest.

Above: Hatch found his niche as a cavalry commander, though had the misfortune of encountering Forrest in 1864.

When Beauregard fired on Fort Sumter, Heintzelman had already served in the Seminole Wars, the Mexican-American War, and the "Cortina Troubles." He led the III Corps of the Army of the Potomac in the Peninsula Campaign and at Second Bull Run. Relieved of command in late 1862, he was later assigned to defend Washington, D.C.

Above: Heintzelman was a victim of the revolving door of generals in the Army of the Potomac.

Helm, Benjamin

(1831–1863) Confederate
Senior position: Brigade commander, Army of
   Tennessee
Final rank: Brigadier General

Heth, Henry "Harry"

(1825–1899) Confederate
Senior position: Division commander, Army of Northern
   Virginia
Final rank: Major General

Helm was a Kentucky politician, attorney, and brother-in-law to Abraham Lincoln, who offered him the job of Union Army paymaster. Helm declined, instead returning to his state to raise the 1st Kentucky Cavalry—for the Confederates. He commanded Kentucky's "Orphan Brigade" during the Tullahoma campaign and was killed while leading his men in a charge at the Battle of Chickamauga.

Best known for errors of judgment, Heth (whom Lee called by his first name) graduated last in his West Point class. He led a "demonstration" against Cincinnati; attacked without reserves at Chancellorsville; and, against orders, initiated the Battle of Gettysburg, where he was wounded. He surrendered with Lee at Appomattox and went into the insurance business.

Above: Helm's death, mourned by Mary Lincoln, helped bring the tragic nature of the Civil War home to the White House.

Above: Heth may have been more valuable to the Army of Northern Virginia for his dedication than his skill at command.

Hill, Ambrose Powell

(1825–1865) Confederate
Senior position: Corps commander,
Army of Northern Virginia
Final rank: Lieutenant General

Born at Culpepper, Hill grew up in a town that lay on the fringes of the Civil War in Virginia. He graduated from West Point in 1847 and served in Mexico, the Third Seminole War, and on the frontier. Hill resigned from the U.S. Army on March 1, 1861, and shortly afterward entered the Confederate service as colonel of the 13th Virginia Infantry. He later grumbled about his unhappy experience of being held in reserve during the battle of First Manassas.

Appointed brigadier general on February 26, 1862, Hill moved south with General Joe Johnston's army and fought his brigade brilliantly at Williamsburg during the Peninsula campaign. Promoted major general on May 26, Hill proved himself a "tower of strength" as he led his division at Mechanicsville, Gaines's Mill, and Frayser's Farm during the Seven Days.

Known as "Hill's Light Division" for its marching speed, the unit became part of Stonewall Jackson's corps after a quarrel erupted between Hill and Longstreet. Under Jackson, Hill served with distinction at Cedar Mountain, Second Manassas and Harpers Ferry. At Antietam it was the rapid march of Hill's Light Division from Harpers Ferry that reinforced Lee in time to repel Burnside's

assault.

After Jackson suffered a mortal wound at Chancellorsville, he turned the command over to Hill. Wounded soon afterward, Hill turned the command over to J. E. B. Stuart. Promoted lieutenant general on May

Above: Unfortunately, contemporary photos of Hill fail to depict his famous red "battle shirt."

24, 1863, Hill assumed command of the newly established III Corps, which he directed on the first day's fighting

Above: Captured Federal wounded during the Seven Days, in which A. P. Hill excelled.
Left: Hill commanded the III Corps throughout most of the Wilderness campaign.

at Gettysburg and through most of the Wilderness campaign of 1864.

During the latter campaigns, Hill began to perplex Lee, who realized that while he performed as a great division commander, he did not perform well as a corps commander, being "too restless and impetuous in action." Lee believed he suffered from a health ailment, and on two occasions Hill took brief leaves but always returned. While attempting to reach his troops with a lone orderly during the defense of the Petersburg lines on April 2, 1865, Hill died from a bullet fired by a Federal straggler.

Hill, Daniel Harvey

(1821–1889) Confederate
Senior position: Corps commander, Army of Tennessee
Final rank: Major General

forcing George Thomas to call for so many reinforcements that his army's right was fatally weakened.

Hill did not serve long under Bragg before he realized that his commanding general lacked strategic and tactical savvy. Perhaps unaware that Jefferson Davis and Bragg were close friends, Hill wrote the war department recommending Bragg's removal from command for incompetence. Instead of recalling Bragg, Davis revoked Hill's commission to lieutenant general and relieved him. Because Congress was in adjournment, Hill continued to serve as lieutenant general until October 23, 1863, when he reverted to major general.

Reducing Hill in grade and leaving him with a small, unimportant command deprived the Confederacy of a competent general. The imbroglio with Bragg, however, was not Hill's first. During the Antietam campaign he had lost a copy of Special Order No. 191 revealing Lee's plans, and refused to admit it.

Left: One of the Confederacy's top generals early in the war, D. H. Hill's acerbic personality won him few friends.
Below: Irish Brigade soldiers killed by Confederates at Antietam, during which battle Daniel Hill was a Rebel commander.

Harvey Hill (he preferred his middle name) opened his fighting career by defeating bungling Ben Butler at Big Bethel on June 10, 1861. He then rose rapidly in the ranks, becoming a major general in March 1862, and making a positive impression as a commander at Seven Pines, the Seven Days' battles, South Mountain, and Antietam. Promoted lieutenant general in July 1863, Hill received orders to take over a corps in Bragg's Army of Tennessee. At Chickamauga, Hill put heavy pressure on the Union left,

Hindman, Thomas C.

(1828–1868) Confederate
Senior position: Commander, Trans-Mississippi
    Department
Final rank: Major General

Hoke, Robert F.

(1837–1912) Confederate
Senior position: Division Commander, Army of
    Northern Virginia
Final rank: Major General

A "fire eater," avowed sectionalist, and one of numerous lawyer-politicians who attained command, Hindman recruited troops and led them from Arkansas to Virginia. Wounded on several occasions, he stumbled when given a significant opportunity to destroy a Federal army near Prairie Grove, Arkansas—the usually audacious man turned cautious. Hindman was assassinated after the war while sitting at home; his murderers were never caught.

Above: Hindman gave his name to Fort Hindman, or Arkansas Post, which was reduced by McClernand and Sherman in January 1863.

With no military background, this Carolina businessman climbed rapidly in rank and responsibility. Commended for "coolness, judgment and efficiency" in D. H. Hill's report of the 1861 Battle of Big Bethel, Virginia, he was severely wounded at Fredericksburg. Thus, he missed Lee's Pennsylvania campaign, but returned to fight in Virginia and the Carolinas, where he surrendered with Johnston's army.

Above: Hoke was a diehard of the Army of Northern Virginia, fighting to the end despite his wounds.

Hood, John Bell

(1831–1879) Confederate
Senior position: Commander, Army
   of Tennessee
Final rank: Lieutenant General

A native Kentuckian and graduate of West Point (where he was almost expelled), Hood switched his home to Texas, where he served with the famous U.S. 2nd Cavalry under A. S. Johnston and R. E. Lee in its battles against the Comanches.

In 1862, with the "Texas Brigade" of the Army of Northern Virginia, Hood led one of the most important attacks of the Civil War when he broke the Federal line at Gaines' Mill on the Peninsula. This breakthrough jumpstarted McClellan's retreat during the Seven Days' battles.

Promoted to division command, Hood further distinguished himself at Second Bull Run and Antietam. At Gettysburg, along with Longstreet, he argued against Lee's plan to attack the Federal left head-on. His Texas scouts had reported an open flank behind the Round Tops. But, following orders, he pitched in, suffering a severe arm wound early in the fight. Recovering quickly, he traveled west with Longstreet's corps ten weeks later and played a leading role at Chickamauga, though there he was wounded in a leg, which had to be amputated at the thigh.

Again recovering quickly, he commanded a corps under Joe Johnston during the Atlanta campaign, and in July 1864 succeeded

Above: The "sad-eyed Viking" Hood was only thirty-three when he was promoted to command the Army of Tennessee.

Johnston as the head of the Army of Tennessee in one of the most controversial command moves of the war. Replacing Johnston's Fabian tactics with aggressive ones, he bloodied his army severely against Sherman's dug-in forces.

Afterward, when Sherman turned away to march to the sea, Hood led one final, disastrous strategic offensive into Tennessee. At Spring Hill he was nearly successful in cutting off a portion of the Union army, but was then "wrathful as a rattlesnake" after hearing the enemy troops had marched past him in the dark. The next day, he launched his men across open fields against Federal breastworks at Franklin in a horrific battle that practically gutted his army.

Stumbling on toward Nashville, Hood sat his weakened army for two weeks until George Thomas assembled enough strength to destroy it, which he did in mid-December. Only a shadow of the once-vaunted Army of Tennessee made it back to Alabama.

Though he was a brilliant brigade and division commander, Hood's performance as an army commander diminished his reputation. Alone among senior commanders, he failed to realize the evolution of defensive tactics that had occurred during the war.

Left: A stylized portrait showing Jeff Davis surrounded by military luminaries of the Confederacy, including Hood, second left..

Hooker, Joseph

(1814–1879) Federal
Senior position: Commander, Army of the Potomac
Final rank: Major General

Hooker came from a military family dating back to the Revolution and readily obtained an appointment to West Point. Graduating in 1837, he demonstrated excellent qualities of leadership during the Mexican War and won brevets to lieutenant colonel while fighting under Zachary Taylor and Winfield Scott. No other lieutenant surpassed Hooker's record for brevets in Mexico, but he soon squabbled with Scott and resigned to become a farmer.

Before the outbreak of the rebellion Hooker applied for a commission but was snubbed by the war depart-

Above: Hooker was dismissed as commander of the Army of the Potomac just three days before Gettysburg.

ment. Finally, on May 17, 1861, he received a brigadier general's commission but saw little action until the Peninsula campaign. Boosted to division command, Hooker proved his fighting abilities in every battle on the Peninsula from Yorktown to Malvern Hill. He won the praise of McClellan and promotion to major general. During the campaign a reporter sent a telegram titled "Fighting—Joe Hooker" as a sub-head, and the clip appeared in the northern press as "Fighting Joe Hooker." The sobriquet embarrassed Hooker for the rest of his life. At Confederate headquarters, Lee mirthfully referred to him as "F.J. Hooker."

Hooker continued to perform well at Second Manassas, South Mountain, and Antietam. At Fredericksburg he led Burnside's Center Grand Division, consisting of the II and III Corps. Behind the scenes and not too quietly he used a few choice invectives accusing his superior of incompetence. Burnside responded by putting Hooker's name at the top of a list of

generals he wanted relieved. Instead, Lincoln relieved Burnside and with some misgivings put Hooker in charge of the Army of the Potomac.

Defeated during the battle of Chancellorsville, Hooker proved no more capable of leading the Army of the Potomac than Burnside. Being knocked unconscious by an exploding shell did not help. Suspected of drinking heavily during the days prior to Gettysburg, and constantly arguing over strategy with the president, Hooker lost his command on June 28, 1863, and was replaced by General Meade. Fighting Joe served the balance of the war doing what he did best, commanding a corps in the west. After the war, Hooker remained in the army and retired in 1868 after suffering a paralytic stroke.

Left: Hooker effectively closed down the Balloon Corps in early 1863, though it was becoming useful in aerial observation.
Below: Hooker fought with Grant's army to defeat Pemberton's Rebels in the Battle of Champion Hill, May 16, 1863.

Howard, Oliver O.

(1830–1909) Federal
Senior position: Commander, Army of the Tennessee
Final rank: Major General

A well-educated and religious "Mainer," Howard had his right arm shattered and amputated following the Battle of Fair Oaks in 1862, where

Left: Howard suffered more than one disaster, but his stellar character caused him to continually be promoted.

Above: Posing with Sherman and his other generals, Howard (at left), is seen without the arm he lost at Fair Oaks on the Peninsula.

he commanded an infantry brigade. General Phil Kearney, whose left arm was amputated, famously joked that the two could shop for gloves together. In 1893, Howard was awarded the Medal of Honor for heroism at Fair Oaks.

Taking over the XI Corps from the inept Franz Sigel in November 1862, Howard stubbornly refused to heed Hooker's warnings to secure his right flank at Chancellorsville. This cost the Union dearly when Stonewall Jackson attacked late in the day, routing Howard's corps. The next year at Gettysburg, he quarreled with Hancock, Meade's designated on-site commander, and initially deployed his men poorly before taking strong defensive positions on Cemetery Hill.

Howard fought under Grant at Chattanooga in 1863, and then was elevated to command of the Army of the Tennessee during the Atlanta campaign. He ultimately commanded the right wing of Sherman's "March to the Sea," which cut the Confederacy in half.

Following the war he helped found Howard University, subdued Chief Joseph and the Nez Perce, and remained on active duty in the army until 1894.

Hurlbut, Stephen A.
(1815–1882) Federal
Senior position: Commander, Army of the Gulf
Final rank: Major General

Huger, Benjamin
(1805–1877) Confederate
Senior position: Division commander, Army of Northern Virginia
Final rank: Major General

Hurlbut was a rare Southerner who remained with the Union. A lawyer and politician, he took readily to command: a division at Shiloh, a corps under Sherman, and eventually the Army of the Gulf. Following the war, he founded the Grand Army of the Republic, served as a U.S. Representative from Illinois and as minister to Colombia and Peru.

A career soldier with artillery experience in the Mexican-American War, Huger was perhaps more qualified as an ordnance officer than a troop commander. Confederate President Jefferson Davis gave him an infantry division—and Lee took it away, apparently for lackluster leadership. Huger finished the war in ordnance positions and retired to become a farmer.

Above: Not a great battle commander, Hurlbut proved an adept administrator in a number of posts.

Above: Huger's greatest failure occurred on the Peninsula, when he had a chance to cut McClellan off before he reached Malvern Hill.

Imboden, John D.

(1823–1895) Confederate
Senior position: Brigade commander, Army of Northern Virginia
Final rank: Brigadier General

Lawyer, teacher, and state legislator, Imboden was praised by Lee for his cavalry heroics. Leading cavalry, artillery, infantry, and partisan irregulars, Imboden proved to be a brave and resourceful officer. Most notably, he covered Lee's retreat after the Battle of Gettysburg. Incapacitated by typhoid fever in 1864, he left cavalry service to supervise Confederate prisoner of war camps.

Above: A dashing officer, first in artillery and then cavalry, Imboden continued to serve even after taking ill.

Jackson, Thomas Jonathan "Stonewall"

(1824–1863) Confederate
Senior position: Corps commander, Army of Northern Virginia
Final rank: Lieutenant General

Raised by his uncle after his parents died, Jackson received a rudimentary education, leaving him far behind his classmates on entering West Point. Through sheer determination his grades improved each year and in 1846 he gradu-

Above: The legendary "Stonewall," whose death in 1863 might also have signaled the demise of the Confederacy.

Above: The Battle of Gaines' Mill, a Confederate victory despite the fact that Jackson arrived late, for the second time during the Seven Days' battles.

ated seventeenth in a class of fifty-nine. Brother cadets admitted "that if the course had been a year longer he would have come out first."

With the Mexican War underway, Second Lieutenant Jackson accompanied John Magruder's battery ashore at Veracruz. During the campaigns at Cerro Gordo and Chapultepec, Jackson received praise from General Winfield Scott and returned home brevetted major. The peacetime army bored him and he joined the staff at the Virginia Military Institute as professor of artillery and natural philosophy. He married and became a devout Presbyterian. The influence of predestination took hold of his life. His personal habits changed, and he never smoked, drank, swore, or played cards.

On April 21, 1861, four days after Virginia seceded from the Union, Jackson reported to Richmond with his militia. Promoted colonel, he went to Harpers Ferry to mobilize troops, dismantle the town's Federal armory and arsenal, and forward the musket-making machinery to Richmond. Jackson went a step further. He ingeniously trapped the Baltimore & Ohio's rolling stock, sent the locomotives to Winchester, and burned the freight cars. When Joe Johnston

arrived at Harpers Ferry to take charge of the district, Jackson had already formed hundreds of recruits into companies and regiments. In the months ahead, those men became Jackson's foot cavalry.

Now a brigadier general, Jackson established his reputation as a fighter at First Manassas, when he rushed his men onto Henry House Hill and repulsed the Federal assault. Fighting nearby, General Bee rallied his brigade by pointing to Jackson, whose men were fighting, formed "like a stone wall." On that day General Jackson became "Stonewall" Jackson.

Above: The ruins of Gaines' Mill on the Peninsula, after the Confederates finally caved in the Union's V Corps.

His men called him "Old Blue Light," because his bluish eyes glittered in battle.

Promoted to major general and

placed in command of the Shenandoah Valley in 1861, Jackson never hit his stride as a commander until the spring of 1862. In his first engagement the Stonewall Brigade suffered heavy loss at Kernstown, but he diverted three Federal armies from joining McClellan's force. In one of the classic campaigns of the war, he defeated General Banks at Front Royal, General Shields at Port Republic—which kept General Irvin McDowell from moving on Fredericksburg—and General

Above: Stonewall Jackson had orders from Lee to march to White Oak Swamp and engage the Union forces there, but he arrived late, again….

Frémont at Cross Keys.
Summoned to Richmond, Jackson

arrived in time for the Seven Days battles but fatigue and unfamiliar terrain brought him to Mechanicsville late. He fought well at Gaines' Mill and pursued McClellan to White Oak Swamp until physical exhaustion overcame his entire division.

Two months later Jackson's foot soldiers covered fifty-one miles in two days and shocked General Pope at Manassas Junction. Jackson took a defensive position at Groveton and on August 28–29, 1862, held off Pope's entire army. After Longstreet arrived, Pope's Army of Virginia disintegrated and fled back to Washington.

Lee now saw an open road to Maryland. He detached Jackson's division, which marched to Harpers Ferry and captured 12,500 Federals before marching through the night to join Lee at Antietam. Despite fatigue, Jackson arrived in time to save Lee from being overwhelmed by superior forces. Promoted lieutenant general, Jackson took command of the II Corps.

Lee retired to Fredericksburg, and Jackson placed his corps on the Army of Northern Virginia's right wing. When on December 13 the Battle of Fredericksburg began, Jackson's corps thwarted an attempt by the Federals to turn his flank. The battle resulted in a great slaughter of Federal troops.

After Fredericksburg, Jackson took leave to spend time with his wife and daughter. He received an urgent call from General Lee on April 29, 1863, when 134,000 Federals under General Joseph Hooker began crossing the Rappahannock River. Jackson arrived on the field and divided his corps, placing half across from Fredericksburg and taking the other half into the Wilderness. While the right wing held the Federals at bay, Jackson marched a circuitous route through the Wilderness. He struck Hooker's right flank on the afternoon of May 2 and relentlessly drove the Federals back towards Chancellorsville.

When dusk fell, Jackson moved into the woods to reconnoiter and fell mortally wounded, accidentally shot by his own men. With his wife beside him on May 10, he said, "Let us cross over the river, and rest under the shade of the trees." Then he died. When Lee received news of Jackson's death, he groaned, "I know not how to replace him." Two months later Lee explained his defeat at Gettysburg when he said, "Jackson is not here."

Jackson, William H. ("Red")

(1835–1903) Confederate
Senior position: Division commander, Army of Mississippi
Final rank: Major General

"Red" Jackson found himself in good company during one of Sherman's rants to Halleck, when he said that Confederate cavalry were "the most dangerous set of men which this war has turned loose upon the world. . . . Stuart, John Morgan, Forrest, and Jackson are the types and leaders of this class." Jackson fought throughout the war, notably around Vicksburg and during the Atlanta campaign. He then joined Hood's ill-fated invasion of Tennessee, and finished his fighting while trying to come to Forrest's aid for the defense of Selma.

Above: A talented, though underrated, cavalry leader, Red Jackson became known for raising thoroughbred horses after the war.

Johnson, Bushrod R.

(1817–1880) Confederate
Senior position: Division commander, Army of Northern Virginia
Final rank: Major General

A soldier and teacher, Johnson fought in the Seminole and Mexican Wars. He twice walked away from disaster, once following Fort Donelson's fall in 1862, where he commanded a wing of the army; then when his division was shattered at Sayler's Creek in 1865. Following the war, he returned to teaching and retired to an Illinois farm.

Above: An excellent fighter, Johnson distinguishing himself in both eastern and western theaters.

Johnson, Edward

(1816–1873) Confederate
Senior position: Division Commander, Army of Northern Virginia
Final rank: Major General

There was no question that "Allegheny" Johnson was a fighter. He fought the Seminoles, the Mexicans, the Indians, and then the Yankees. Seriously wounded once, he fought through the war from 1861 to December 1864, when he was captured for the second time. Lee trusted him; Ewell missed him; Hood used him. After the war, Johnson retired to a farm in Virginia.

Above: Johnson was swinging his cane at a swarm of Federals just before he was captured at Spotsylvania's "Bloody Angle."

Johnston, Albert Sidney

(1805–1862) Confederate
Senior position: Commander, Army of Mississippi
Final rank: General

Above Considered by some, including Jefferson Davis, to be the best soldier on the continent, A. S. Johnston died at Shiloh, perhaps changing the course of the war.

A close friend of Jefferson Davis and an 1826 graduate of West Point, Johnston stood on a pedestal within the early Confederacy as being the South's foremost field commander. He had established a brilliant reputation in the Texas revolutionary army, served as secretary of war for the Republic of Texas, and fought with distinction at Monterrey in the Mexican War. He then rejoined the U.S. Army and in 1855 became colonel of the 2nd Cavalry. In 1857 he led the Utah expedition against the Mormons and earned a brevet to brigadier general for another brilliant performance.

At the outset of the rebellion Stanley F. Horn, who wrote *The Army of Tennessee*, said, "If there was any one thing on which everyone seemed agreed in 1861 it was that Albert Sidney Johnston was the Number One soldier on the continent." Jefferson Davis certainly agreed, declaring, "If Sidney Johnston is not a general . . . we have no general." He quickly boosted Johnston to full general on August 31, 1861, to rank from May 30, 1861, and put him in charge of all Confederate territory from the Appalachians in the east to the Indian Territory in the west.

Johnston immediately adopted the president's strategy of defending all points of the Confederacy with isolated detachments. The failures of the officers he put in charge became

by surprise and initiated a bloody, two-day battle at Shiloh. Confused by thick woods and unfamiliar terrain, Johnston's men struggled before turning the Federal left. Leading the attack near a peach orchard around 2:00 P.M., Johnston suffered a wound in the leg that bled out and took his life. Despite those in the Confederacy who referred to Johnston's death as a "catastrophe," Grant considered him overrated, and though bold in his concepts, "vacillating and undecided in his actions."

Left: Johnston is said to have dispatched his personal physician to help a wounded Federal soldier, while he himself bled to death from a shot in the leg.

Johnston, Joseph Eggleston

(1807–1891) Confederate
Senior position: Commander,
  Department of the West
Final rank: General

Born in Farmville, Virginia, Johnston graduated from West Point in 1829, thirteenth in a class of forty-six that also included Robert E. Lee, who graduated second. Johnston chose the artillery and spent most of his early years pulling garrison duty in the

Right: Considered by some to be a better general than Lee, Joe Johnston's removal from command during the Atlanta campaign still causes controversy.

manifest in early 1862 with the loss of forts Henry and Donelson followed by most of Kentucky and Tennessee. Johnston withdrew into northern Mississippi and concentrated his army with General Beauregard's forces near Corinth.

On April 6, 1862, Johnston attempted to justify the president's confidence by striking Grant's forces *en masse* at Pittsburg Landing on the Tennessee River. The assault caught the Federals

Above: A truce on Kennesaw Mountain, in contrast to the horrendously bloody action as Sherman tried unsuccessfully to dislodge Joe Johnston's well dug-in Rebels.

west. He resigned from the army in 1837 to become a civil engineer in Florida. Attacked by Seminoles and wounded, he led an orderly retreat and rejoined the army as a first lieutenant.

Wounded five times during the Mexican War, Johnston won three brevets and led the assault on Chapultepec. After serving on the frontier, he returned to Washington on June 28, 1860, as quartermaster general with the rank of brigadier general. Ten months later he resigned and joined the Confederacy.

He was commissioned a brigadier general in the Confederate army on May 14, 1861, and took command of the forces at Harpers Ferry, where Stonewall Jackson had been dismantling the Federal armory. Finding the area suitable for neither offense nor defense, Johnston moved the army into the Shenandoah Valley, where for several weeks he baffled General Robert Patterson's Pennsylvania militia. When General Beauregard faced attack at First Manassas (Bull Run), Johnston moved his force by rail, took command of the battlefield, and routed the Federal army.

On August 31, 1861, President Davis rewarded Johnston's performance at First Manassas by promoting him general to rank from July 4, and naming him commander of the Department of the Potomac. Being ranked fourth behind Samuel Cooper, Albert Sidney Johnston, and Robert E. Lee resulted in an acrimonious relationship with Davis, which over time did great disservice to the Confederacy. Johnston had been the senior officer in the U.S. Army and believed he should retain the same seniority in the Confederate army, and his feud with Davis continued *ad nauseam*.

During McClellan's 1862 Peninsula campaign, Johnston rushed forces from Fredericksburg and took control of the battlefield. He staged brilliant defensive movements until May 30, when wounded twice at Seven Pines. Relieved by General Lee on June 1, 1862, Johnston returned to duty in November to command the Department of the West, which included Bragg's army in Tennessee and Pemberton's army in Mississippi. Davis disapproved Johnston's strategy of combining forces and imposed his own. The error eventually led to Pemberton's defeat at Vicksburg and to Bragg's misfortunes at Stones River, Tullahoma, and Chattanooga.

Johnston understood the weaknesses of the Confederate army and believed the South might outlast the North by conserving its resources and fighting defensively. This was not the attitude of Davis when in December 1863 he relieved Bragg and put Johnston in charge of the Army of Tennessee with orders to reorganize the force and assume the offensive.

Johnston knew better and followed his own strategy.

When General Sherman commenced the Atlanta campaign

Below: While Johnston tried persuading his fellow officer, Pemberton, to abandon Vicksburg, Grant tried other methods—assaults supported by heavy artillery fire.

Above: Joe Johnston specialized in defensive tactics, which may have served the Confederacy better than offensive ones.

during the spring of 1864, Johnston fought an exceptionally skillful retreat against an overwhelmingly superior Federal army. Disgruntled by Johnston's reluctance to take the offensive as Sherman's army converged on Atlanta, Davis replaced him on July 17, 1864, and turned the army over to General Hood, an aggressive commander with little tactical finesse. Hood proved his ineptness by fighting recklessly at Atlanta and even more recklessly at Franklin and Nashville. Johnston could do nothing but painfully watch while privately castigating Davis for military incompetence.

Johnston saw no more action until February 1865, when Lee assumed overall command of the Confederate army. Well aware of Johnston's talents, Lee pulled him out of imposed inactivity and on February 23 put him in charge of the ad hoc forces gathering to oppose Sherman's march through the Carolinas. Once again with only a small force, Johnston deftly retreated while preventing Sherman's army from moving north and merging with Grant's army at Petersburg. When President Davis fled from Richmond with his cabinet in early April, he ordered Johnston south to continue the war and to provide a bodyguard. Johnston owed Davis no favors and gave none. On April 26 he surrendered to Sherman seventeen days after Lee surrendered at Appomattox.

As might be expected, long debates ensued after the war regarding Johnston's ability as a commander. Some contemporaries pegged him as a superb defensive tactician and at least the equal of Lee, but without having other attributes necessary in a commander. Douglas Southall Freeman, whose opinion probably trumped all, spoke of Johnston's "unmistakable strategical sense" but felt he lacked administrative ability. "A difficult and touchy subordinate he is," wrote Freeman, "though a generous and kindly superior—in sum, a military contradiction and a temperamental enigma."

Kearny, Philip
(1815–1862) Federal
Senior position: Division commander, Army of the Potomac
Final rank: Major General

Kearny saw enough of war in Europe and Mexico to last a lifetime. A decorated cavalryman, the wealthy New Yorker—the bravest and most perfect soldier," said General-In-Chief Winfield Scott—lost an arm during the Mexican-American War. Lincoln considered him for command of all Union armies, but Kearny was killed at the Battle of Chantilly in 1862.

Right: Famous before the war for his Indian fighting, Kearny died at Chantilly, and both sides mourned.

Kershaw, Joseph B.

(1822–1894) Confederate
Senior position: Division commander, Army of Northern Virginia
Final rank: Major General

Leading volunteer infantry, Kershaw participated in the 1861 Battle of Bull Run. He subsequently fought through Gettysburg and, when Longstreet's corps was transferred west, saw action at Chickamauga. Returning east, he was in the fighting at the Wilderness, Spotsylvania, and Cold Harbor. Captured at Sayler's Creek in 1865, the South Carolinian eventually returned to politics and his law practice.

Above: A stalwart of the Army of Northern Virginia, Kershaw was fortunate to have survived the war.

Kilpatrick, Hugh Judson

(1836–1881) Federal
Senior position: Division commander, Military Division
of Mississippi
Final rank: Major General

An 1861 West Point graduate, Kilpatrick was the first regular Union army officer to be wounded. Hit seriously twice, he nevertheless served the entire war—occasionally with distinction and courage. A New Jersey native, Kilpatrick was audacious and ambitious, never hesitating to use political influence and his troopers for personal gain. Cavalrymen referred to him as "Kill-Cavalry" for his reckless disregard of their lives. His camps were shabby, and he could often be found in his cot with a prostitute. Jailed on corruption charges in 1862, he was accused of selling captured goods and pocketing the proceeds. He was jailed again for a drunken spree in Washington, and for (allegedly) accepting bribes in the procurement of horses.

Still, Judson Kilpatrick was a fighter. He participated in numerous cavalry raids to destroy railroads and supply depots. After a failed spring raid in 1864, the infamous

"Kilpatrick-Dahlgren Raid," after which he admitted that his objective was to kill Jefferson Davis and his cabinet, not to liberate Federal prisoners, he was forced to transfer to Sherman's western command. There his capacity for destroying property was tested in the "March to the Sea." Sherman said, "I know that Kilpatrick is a hell of a damned fool, but I want just that sort of man to command my cavalry on this expedition."

In North Carolina, while sleeping with a local belle, he was surprised by Confederate cavalry and barely escaped, though without his trousers. Following the war, Kilpatrick entered politics, without success, and served as U.S. Minister to Chile.

Right: A raucous, reckless character, Kilpatrick nevertheless participated in some of the more dashing exploits of the war.
Below: One of Kilpatrick's plans was to free Union PoWs from Libby Prison—and to assassinate Jefferson Davis and the Confederate cabinet.

Lee, Fitzhugh

(1835–1905) Confederate
Senior position: Division commander, Army of Northern Virginia
Final rank: Major General

Law, Evander M.

(1836–1920) Confederate
Senior position: Division commander, Army of Northern Virginia
Final rank: Major General

Leading from the front, this teacher was shot on multiple occasions while leading his Alabama Zouaves from the First Battle of Bull Run in 1861, through Gettysburg in July and Chickamauga in September 1863. Quarreling with other generals, he was arrested for insubordination, was severely wounded at Cold Harbor, and surrendered with Johnston's army after the Battle of Bentonville in 1865.

Above: Law simply wouldn't stop fighting, until the major armies of the Confederacy had laid down their arms.

A nephew of Robert E. Lee, Fitzhugh Lee was related to signers of the Declaration of Independence and American heroes in all theaters of politics, commerce, and the military. Upon graduating from West Point, his first battles were against the Comanche in Texas, where he was severely wounded.

An exceptional commander of cavalry, Lee fought with Jeb Stuart and under Wade Hampton after Stuart was

Above: A talented cavalry leader, Fitzhugh Lee capably stepped into big shoes after Jeb Stuart was killed.

killed. At Chancellorsville in May 1863, Lee demonstrated the cavalry's perfect role in 19th century warfare when his reconnaissance discovered the unsecured right flank of Hooker's army. This allowed Stonewall Jackson to cave in the flank—a movement led by Lee's cavalry—to win the field for the Confederacy.

In "after-action" reports following the battle of Gettysburg, Stuart wrote that Lee was "one of the finest cavalry leaders on the continent, and richly [entitled] to promotion." When he was a major general, his troopers fought Sheridan in the Shenandoah Valley where he was wounded at the Battle of Third Winchester. Lee ultimately led the final cavalry charge of the Confederacy on April 9, 1865, prior to the settlement at Appomattox.

A planter, Lee served as governor of Virginia, remained aloof from the "Lost Cause" paranoia that swept the southern states, and eventually served honorably in the Spanish-American War.

Lee, Robert Edward

(1807–1870) Confederate
Senior position: Commander of the Armies of the Confederacy
Final rank: General

Above: Lee when he was a colonel in the U.S. Army.
Right: Robert E. Lee flanked by (on his right) his eldest son, G. W. C. Lee, and Colonel Walter Taylor, aide to the Confederate leader, photographed in 1865.
Following pages: The Battle of Cold Harbor, May 21 to June 12, 1864, was the final victory won by Lee's army.

An irony of the Civil War is that although the North triumphed—for a cause which is now universally considered superior—the most honored military commander to emerge from the conflict was a general of the South: Robert E. Lee.

A tragic figure in some respects, Lee was one of the most respected soldiers in the country prior to the war, and was even offered command of the Union armies. But he could not turn his hand against Virginia, and so fought for a cause that he recognized had little chance of winning, but which honor could not let him relinquish. During the course of the war his humanity was as apparent as his military skills, and his final surrender may well have marked the passing of an entire era of chivalry.

Lee was the son of "Light Horse Harry" Lee, a hero of the Revolution, and he established an estate in Arlington, which is now the national cemetery. Related by birth and marriage to some of America's top families, Robert proved his own worth through service in the Mexican War and against the Indians, and was also a superintendent of West Point.

Early in the Civil War, however, Lee was not so admired. First assigned to some fruitless efforts in western Virginia, he was then sent south to oversee coastal defenses. For his seeming devotion to defensive preparations, Richmond newspapers derisively called him the "King of Spades." It was not until Joe Johnston was wounded at the Battle of Seven Pines that Lee took over the Army of Northern Virginia, thence to meet his destiny as one of history's great commanders.

"Audacity" was the word that soon described Lee, as he

army to open a third front—this was Stonewall Jackson's famous flank march that crushed Joe Hooker's right.

After this latest victory, Lee decided to carry the war to the North once more, this time to Pennsylvania. At the Battle of Gettysburg, following Jackson's death, Lee was unable to find the "cordial cooperation" he desired from his subordinates. Historians have long debated whether his considerate language when issuing orders reflected a certain weakness. Undisputed is the fact that when Lee's army invaded the North, his troops were under strict orders not to disturb civilian property. This stands in clear contrast to Sherman's and Sheridan's later invasions of the South.

After Gettysburg the Army of the Potomac was quiescent for nearly a year, but then in the spring of 1864 Grant took over and initiated a series of horrific attacks at the Wilderness, Spotsylvania, and Cold Harbor. Lee fended off the assaults until Grant was able to pin the Confederates down at the crucial rail center of Petersburg. Lee had finally been forced into the situation he'd dreaded: a protracted siege, which he knew the resources of the Confederacy could not support.

At the start of April 1865, after Lee had made one last attempt to break the siege, he was forced to abandon both Petersburg and Richmond. For a week, he led his army to the west, hoping to continue the fight, but Federal infantry and cavalry swarmed around him, blocking his escape. At Appomattox Court House on April 9, Lee finally agreed to the surrender of his famished, diminished army.

After the war, Lee became president of Washington College (now called Washington and Lee). It has been regretted ever since that he never wrote a memoir; however it is known from his statements, both during the war and after, that he never sought to cast blame or responsibility on anyone but himself, no matter how badly people had failed him. Or as he said at the Battle of Gettysburg, after the final Confederate charge had failed, "It is all my fault."

took the initiative against superior Federal forces under McClellan, forcing them through the Seven Days' battles to evacuate the Peninsula. He then turned north to demolish another Union army, under Pope, at Second Bull Run. Following this victory he sought to remove the war from Virginia's soil by carrying it to Maryland, where he expected to find fresh recruits, supplies, and enthusiasm.

Lee was disappointed, however, as the population of that state failed to rally to the Confederacy. Further, McClellan had captured one of his dispatches and had closed in on his forces with an army twice his size. At Antietam Creek Lee stood fast in the bloodiest day in American history. The next day he continued to hold the field until finally recrossing the Potomac back to Virginia.

That December the Army of Northern Virginia repulsed a Union invasion at Fredericksburg, and then another in the spring at Chancellorsville. The latter was perhaps Lee's greatest victory as he was heavily outnumbered and beset on two sides, and yet decided to split his

Lee, Stephen Dill

(1833–1908) Confederate
Senior position: Corps commander, Army of Tennessee
Final rank: Lieutenant General

Lee, William Henry Fitzhugh "Rooney"

(1837–1891) Confederate
Senior position: Division commander, Army of Northern Virginia
Final rank: Major General

As an artillery captain, Lee was present when Fort Sumter fell. He went on to senior commands in artillery, cavalry and infantry, becoming the youngest lieutenant general in the Confederacy. Captured at Vicksburg, he was paroled, fought Sherman in Georgia, commanded a corps under Hood in Tennessee, and surrendered with Joe Johnston in North Carolina. Afterward, he returned to his plantation and became the first president of Mississippi State University.

Above: An exceptional young commander, S. D. Lee sullied his reputation by the headlong attacks he favored at Tupelo and around Atlanta.

"Rooney" Lee was the second son of Robert E. Lee, and a fine commander of cavalry. He was recovering from wounds received during the Gettysburg campaign when captured by Federal troops. Exchanged, he fought through the war's remaining major battles until the surrender at Appomattox. He then returned to his plantation and eventually served in the Virginia Senate and U.S. House of Representatives.

Above: Rooney Lee did his father proud as a cavalry commander, especially during the war's last year.

Longstreet, James

(1821–1904) Confederate
Senior position: Corps commander,
Army of Northern Virginia
Final rank: Lieutenant General

The son of a South Carolina planter, Longstreet had the good fortune of being educated at West Point. He graduated in 1838 with such notables as Ulysses Grant, Henry Halleck, George Thomas, and William T. Sherman. Like many of the young officers from his class, he fought in the Mexican War, earned two brevets, and afterward saw duty on the frontier.

On June 1, 1861, Longstreet resigned from the U.S. Army and applied for a brigadier general's post in the Confederate army as paymaster. He received his commission on June 17 but instead of an administrative job found himself in charge of the Fourth Brigade at Manassas. By demonstrating skillful leadership during the battle, Longstreet moved up to division command and on October 7, 1861, became a major general under Joe Johnston.

During the Peninsula campaign, Longstreet distinguished himself on May 5, 1862, while commanding a stubborn rear guard action at Williamsburg as Johnston set his forces for the defense of Richmond.

Right: Longstreet fell out with his fellow Confederates when he became a Republican after the war, but during it he was the "bulldog" of the Army of Northern Virginia.

Longstreet's luck changed on May 31 when his tardiness to get into position at Seven Pines gave McClellan's Federals control of the battlefield. The fault occurred through a misunderstanding of orders. After Robert E. Lee assumed command, Longstreet quickly redeemed himself during the Seven Days' battles. Lee observed Longstreet's courage, and when he reorganized his forces into the Army of Northern Virginia, he gave Longstreet command of half the infantry.

After Stonewall Jackson began driving General Pope's Federals back to Manassas in August 1862, Longstreet crossed the Rapidan and on the morning of the 29th joined Jackson on the old Bull Run battlefield. Lee expressed disappointment when Longstreet waited until the next day to go on the offensive. Although Longstreet's assault on August 30

Above: Fort Sanders, Knox County, Tennessee, being assaulted by a portion of Longstreet's corps, during what is regarded as the decisive engagement in the Knoxville

routed the Federals, the one-day delay manifested a flaw in the general's behavior when he doubted the wisdom of his superior's orders.

Although Longstreet did not agree with Lee's invasion of Maryland in September 1862, he fought valiantly and skillfully at Antietam. Once again impressed, Lee recommended Longstreet for a lieutenant generalship and grouped his division into the I Corps. The timing could not have been better because on December 13 Longstreet's corps decimated the Federal infantry at Fredericksburg.

On February 17, 1863, Lee detached Longstreet with two divisions and gave him an opportunity to lead an independent command. After Longstreet initiated no action Lee issued direct orders to attack Suffolk. Longstreet complied without enthusiasm in April and wasted nearly a month to little effect.

Following Jackson's death at Chancellorsville in May, Lee's relationship with Longstreet became more intimate. During the Gettysburg campaign Longstreet advocated a defensive position while Lee insisted on aggressively attacking. Ordered to assault the Federal position at dawn on July 2, Longstreet stalled, waiting for one more division to get in position. The assault struck the Union flank around 4:30 P.M. By then the Federals had adjusted their lines, causing enormous Confederate casualties. Longstreet also demonstrated lethargy in mounting Pickett's Charge on the third day, mainly because he disagreed with the plan and by stalling hoped Lee would change his mind. Southerners blamed Longstreet for Lee's defeat at Gettysburg, but as Douglas Southall Freeman concluded, "Lee never gave any intimation that he considered Longstreet's failure at Gettysburg

Below: Longstreet on the attack at Gettysburg, Blue Ridge in the distance.

more than the error of a good soldier."

During the autumn of 1863 the Army of the Potomac demonstrated no appetite for fighting, so Lee detached Longstreet and sent him to Georgia to reinforce General Bragg. Longstreet fought well at Chickamauga but in November made little progress against Burnside's fortifications at Knoxville. Feeling downcast, he considered resigning. Lee could not afford to lose Longstreet and summoned him back to the Army of Northern Virginia. Longstreet's leading division arrived on May 6, 1864, just in time to assist A. P. Hill's corps during the second day of the battle of the Wilderness. He organized a brilliant counterattack but suffered a bad wound that incapacitated him until October.

Longstreet returned to the Army of Northern Virginia to command forces in the vicinity of Bermuda Hundred and remained with his corps until the surrender at Appomattox Court House on April 9, 1865. As Southerners began to re-evaluate the defeat at Gettysburg, they became more vehement in blaming Longstreet for losing the turning point of the war. Lee continued to defend Longstreet, whom he called "my old War Horse." Most of Longstreet's men, who affectionately called him "Old Pete," also defended their general. To assess objectively, Longstreet assuredly failed as an independent commander, but he probably had little competition in either army as a battlefield tactician.

Lyon, Nathaniel
(1818–1861) Federal
Senior position: Commander, Army of the West
Final rank: Major General

Above: Lyon seized the initiative early in the war, though it only led to his death rather than further glory in defense of the Union.

Lyon served capably in the Seminole and Mexican Wars, though was accused of massacring defenseless Pomo Indians in California. A hotheaded Unionist, his vigorous defense of Missouri—securing the Federal arsenal in Springfield and dispersing Southern-sympathizing militia at the Battle of Boonville—may have saved that state for the Union, but provoked much bitterness that continued. Shot multiple times, Lyon died during the Battle of Wilson's Creek in August 1861.

Magruder, John B.

(1807–1871) Confederate
Senior position: Commander,
District of Texas, New Mexico,
and Arizona
Final rank: Major General

Mansfield, Joseph K.

(1803–1862) Federal
Senior position: Corps commander,
Army of the Potomac
Final rank: Major General

As a youth, Magruder dined with Thomas Jefferson, and as a seasoned veteran with Mexico's Maximilian I. His brilliant—and cunning—defense of Virginia in 1862 was followed closely by poor performance at the Seven Days' battles. Lee subsequently banned him to the west, where "Prince John" again fought brilliantly in wresting Galveston from a superior Federal force.

Above: The burning of the village of Hampton, Va, by Rebel troops under General Magruder.

Perhaps the oldest general in the Federal forces, Mansfield was a veteran of the Mexican-American War where, as a junior officer, he performed with courage. On the opening day of the battle of Antietam in September 1862, the white-haired general was commanding at the front on horseback, when he and his horse were shot. Mansfield died the fnext day.

Right: Joseph Mansfield cut an impressive figure in uniform, one that Rebel sharpshooters apparently zeroed in on at Antietam.

Marmaduke, John S.

(1833–1887) Confederate
Senior position: Division commander, Trans-Mississippi
  Department
Final rank: Major General

Maury, Dabney H.

(1822–1900) Confederate
Senior position: Commander, Department of the Gulf
Final rank: Major General

Since he was fighting along the Mississippi, eastern newspapers tended to miss Marmaduke's victories and defeats. The son and grandson of state governors, he fought at Shiloh and defended Louisiana from invasion. When he stated that his superior, Lucius Walker, had shirked his duty, Walker challenged him to a duel—and lost. Captured in Missouri, Marmaduke eventually became that state's governor.

Above: A good fighter, Marmaduke damaged his career by dueling with a fellow officer, causing a casualty the Confederacy could not afford.

When war began, this Virginian was a veteran of battles from Mexico to Oregon. Hearing news of Fort Sumter's fall, he joined the Confederate army. Maury was a competent officer and served in numerous capacities, from aide-de-camp to field commander, and participated in the battles of Vicksburg, Corinth, and Mobile. After the war, he taught classical literature and mathematics.

Above: Maury commanded the garrison at Mobile at the end of the war, and provided good service afterward with incisive writings.

McClellan, George B.

(1826–1885) Federal
Senior position: Commander-in-
Chief, U.S. Army
Final rank: Major General

After graduating second in his 1846 West Point class, George McClellan's first combat was in the Mexican War. Joining Winfield Scott's army later that year, he carried a double-barreled shotgun, two pistols, a saber, dress sword, and a Bowie knife—ready to fight, it seemed. He won two brevets and acquitted himself well.

During the 1850s he surveyed ports and railroad lines, and was sent to South America, Europe and the Crimea as a military observer. Despite the lavish attention the handsome young officer enjoyed abroad, he resigned from the army and became a railroad executive.

When the Civil War broke out, governors in both North and South courted McClellan, who, it was thought, understood "the big picture." With no experience handling troops, the charming—some said charismatic—captain was commissioned a major general of Ohio Volunteers. He had no problems with slavery, he said, but he opposed secession.

McClellan had immediate success in enabling the western counties of Virginia to break from their state and, following McDowell's miserable performance at Bull Run, Lincoln made him overall army commander. McClellan came to believe that he could rescue the nation and that

anyone who opposed him was either incompetent or a traitor. In the desperate circumstances of 1861, while organizing the Army of the Potomac, he undermined Winfield Scott and the old general was removed, leaving McClellan in sole command. Uncomfortable with this situation, in March 1862 Lincoln arranged to restrict McClellan to command of the Army of the Potomac

Above: President Lincoln and McClellan discuss the progress of the war in the general's tent at Antietam, 1862.
Following pages: The action swirls around Dunker Church, on the battlefield of Antietam,

rather than all armies in the field.

With a tendency to dramatically overestimate Confederate strength, McClellan moved cautiously. His ultimate plan emerged as the Peninsula Campaign, which after many weeks of creeping progress finally established the Union army within five miles of Richmond. But then Robert E. Lee launched the Seven Days' battles to drive McClellan back, ultimately all the way to Washington. Convinced that he'd been betrayed by his superiors,

McClellan managed to be miles away from the actual fighting, busy demanding reinforcements and writing accusatory telegrams.

Meanwhile, the administration formed another army under John Pope, but it was routed at Second Bull Run in August 1862. This event was not considered tragic by McClellan and his partisans in the Army of the Potomac. When "Little Mac" rode forth to once again take command a huge cheer went up from the rank and file. His troops, of course, idolized

Above: Shorter than average, McClellan (third from left) looks even more diminutive against Lincoln's lanky frame.

drilling and polishing gear rather than the bloody business of battle. Lincoln, whom McClellan called a meddling baboon, wrote, "If he can't fight himself, he excels in making others ready to fight."

Showing no such reluctance, Robert E. Lee invaded Maryland. McClellan confronted him at Antietam to prompt the bloodiest day in American history. Though McClellan had a two-to-one advantage in manpower, he hesitated to use his entire force, and Antietam ended in a tactical draw. But it did force Lee to return to Virginia, allowed Lincoln to issue his Emancipation Proclamation, and discouraged Britain and France from recognizing the Confederacy.

After failing to pursue Lee, McClellan was removed for good. Lincoln remarked, "If General McClellan does not want to use the army, I would like to borrow it for a time." As the "peace candidate," McClellan opposed Lincoln in the 1864 presidential election, but by then the fortunes of war had turned in the Union's favor. The "Young Napoleon" spent the remaining years of his life as a businessman and politician.

McClernand, John A.

(1812–1900) Federal
Senior position: Corps commander, Army of the Tennessee
Final rank: Major General

Above: McClernand was squeezed out at the first opportunity by Grant, Sherman, and Halleck.
Left: A favorite of Lincoln for political reasons, McClernand (right) is seen here with the president and the detective Alan Pinkerton.

McClernand was the very model of a Northern "political general," since as a pro-war Democrat from Illinois he had more influence with Lincoln than many West Point-trained generals. Despite his lack of martial experience, however, he fought with distinction in some of the fiercest early battles of the war. His first action came at Belmont when he ably led a brigade of Illinois volunteers. At Fort Donelson in February 1862, it was his men who took the brunt when attacking Confederates came streaming out of their works to turn the Federal right. Though his division gave way while suffering over 2,000 casualties, McClernand himself held steady while waiting for support from Grant and the rest of the army. His division was next to Sherman's at Shiloh, and though both units were largely shaken by the Confederate onslaught, the two commanders managed to maintain cohesion, conferring throughout the battle.

The real troubles began when McClernand secured authority from Lincoln to raise an army of his own to take the city of Vicksburg, which was then the project of Grant and Sherman. With the support of Halleck, the West Pointers stood firm, and Sherman launched his ill-fated attack at the Chickasaw Bluffs before McClernand could arrive. Afterward, the Illinois general claimed great credit for seizing Arkansas Post, though Grant considered the effort unnecessary.

During the final battles for Vicksburg, McClernand commanded a corps and again fought bravely, but Grant relieved him of duty for supposed incompetence and for extolling his own command to the press. Lincoln assigned him to another corps command in the Gulf, but ill health forced McClernand to finally resign from the army.

McCook, Alexander M.
(1831–1903) Federal
Senior position: Corps commander, Army of the Cumberland
Final rank: Major General

Above: As much as any Union general, McCook suffered the brunt of the aggressive assaults launched by the Rebel Army of Tennessee.

Ohio's "Fighting McCooks" contributed six generals to the Union. This McCook fought the Apaches and Utes and was an infantry instructor at West Point. Unfortunately, his infantry was routed at Perryville and Stones River in 1862 and at Chickamauga in 1863. Court-martialed, but not convicted, he saw no more service at the front for the remainder of the war.

McDowell, Irvin

(1818–1885) Federal
Senior position: Commander, Army of Northeastern Virginia
Final rank: Major General

An aide-de-camp (military for personal assistant or secretary) to field commanders in the Mexican War and an instructor at West Point, McDowell never commanded troops before he was appointed, through the political influence of friends, commander of Northeastern Virginia. When he was subsequently pressured by those friends to invade and defeat the Confederacy, his inexperienced soldiers were soundly routed at the First Battle of Bull Run (Manassas). McDowell's plan of battle had been sound, but the inability of his untested troops to withstand the Confederate firepower, as well as poor methods of communicating during a battle proved his undoing. After Bull Run, the cautious and politically sensitive George McClellan replaced McDowell as army commander. McDowell was assigned the I Corps and soon posted to defend Washington, D.C.

Transferred to command the III Corps in John Pope's Army of Virginia, he was thoroughly scrutinized for actions contributing to the Union defeat at the Second Battle of Bull Run. When Pope subsequently court-martialed General Fitz-John Porter for insubordination in that battle, McDowell testified against Porter. McDowell's testimony was eventually seen as self-serving and he was accused of perjury. Escaping official blame, he was transferred (exiled) to the Department of the Pacific where he spent the balance of the war.

Above: Though he devised an excellent plan at First Bull Run, McDowell lost the confidence of the public after that first great Union defeat.

McLaws, Lafayette

(1821–1897) Confederate
Senior position: Division commander, Army of Northern Virginia
Final rank: Major General

A professional military officer, the Georgian McLaws alternately pleased and disappointed his commanders because of inconsistent performances. Fighting for both Lee and Longstreet, he was ultimately passed over for command of a corps and relieved of duties for his failure to take Fort Sanders in Knoxville. He spent the remainder of the war in military exile in Georgia.

Above: McLaws looked and fought like a lion at Gettysburg, as elsewhere, though his bravery was not always rewarded by success.

McPherson, James B.

(1828–1864) Federal
Senior position: Commander, Army of the Tennessee
Final rank: Major General

Above: McPherson's death at Atlanta caused Sherman to drop the resentment he held for the Army of the Tennessee's prior failure at Resaca.

Graduating first in his class from the U.S. Military Academy at West Point in 1853, McPherson spent several years working on harbor improvements and fortifications in New York and San Francisco (Alcatraz Island).

When war broke out, however, he immediately requested a transfer to the east and was posted to Halleck's and Grant's armies, which were operating along the Mississippi and Ohio Rivers. As chief engineer at the successful sieges of Fort Donelson and Vicksburg—then thought to be impregnable—he was valued highly by Grant, and promotions to major general commanding the XVII Corps, and then the Army of the Tennessee, followed.

During Sherman's drive into Georgia, McPherson very nearly cut behind Joe Johnston's army with a maneuver that could have ended the campaign in a week, but at the last minute hesitated. Ten weeks later, he and Sherman were discussing tactics near Atlanta when the Confederates launched a huge attack against the Army of the Tennessee's left. Rushing to the scene of battle, McPherson ran into Confederate skirmishers who had broken through. They called on him to surrender, but he just politely tipped his hat and turned to gallop away. He was pierced through the breast by a Confederate bullet and was said to have died instantly. A cheerful, handsome individual, McPherson was deeply mourned, not only by Grant and Sherman, but by the commander of the Confederate army he had died fighting, John Bell Hood, who had been his close friend at West Point.

Meade, George G.

(1815–1872) Federal
Senior position: Commander, Army of the Potomac
Final rank: Major General

A professional military officer in the days when the "best and brightest" were engineers, Meade spent years supervising coastal defenses, including lighthouses, and then

Right: Meade won the greatest Union victory of the war, yet failed to earn the confidence of Lincoln to avoid being placed under Grant.

Above: Meade (right center with saber) poses with his generals.

fought well in the Seminole and Mexican Wars. With political backing, he was promoted from captain to brigadier general of volunteers when the Civil War began, and helped develop the defenses of Washington, including Fort Meade.

Wounded on multiple occasions, Meade commanded his forces—from smaller brigades to divisions to corps—in the Seven Days' battles, Second Bull Run, Antietam, Fredericksburg, and Chancellorsville, serving competently in difficult situations and winning the praise of his superiors.

Meade is best remembered,

however, as the Federal commander in charge when the tide of history turned at Gettysburg. But there was both more to the man and more to the battle than simply winning or losing.

In the early morning of June 28, 1863, with Lee moving aggressively northward, an unidentified officer entered Meade's tent. Meade immediately thought that, caught in the army's perpetual web of intrigue, he was being arrested. Instead the man informed him that he was "Fighting Joe" Hooker's replacement at the head of the Army of the Potomac. Without knowing the disposition, strength or movements of the balance of his army, three days later he faced Lee at Gettysburg.

Gettysburg saw 50,000 men killed and wounded. It was an accidental battle, the results of which determined the fate of the Union and the Confederacy. Meade deployed his forces in strong defensive positions along Cemetery Ridge and Lee hurled thousands of men against the Federal high ground, including one final assault, the disastrous Pickett's Charge, in which the Confederates sustained more than 50 percent casualties.

As Lee withdrew, Meade failed to order a close pursuit and many, including Lincoln, faulted him for allowing the beaten army to escape. The greatest insult, however, was the sniping of politicians supported by two scheming and incompetent Federal generals, Sickles and Butterfield.

Meade operated best in support and defensive roles, however, and when Lincoln promoted Grant to be his superior officer, Meade offered to resign. Grant, however, would not hear of it. He used Meade as commander of an army under his control in 1864–65, enduring Meade's jealousy and defensiveness. Despite their differences, the men worked relatively well together until the end of the war.

Meigs, Montgomery Cunningham

(1816–1892) Federal
Senior position: Quartermaster General
Final rank: Major General

Meigs never believed his talents were fully utilized, but his task was enormous. Through four years of war, he turned a small peacetime quarter-master system into one accommodating an army of a million men. A stickler for honesty, he also fought battles against corruption, improper supply contracts, kickbacks, and scandals while dispensing and accounting for more than $1.5 billion in expenditures.

Above: Serving behind the scenes, Meigs' contribution to the Union war effort exceeded that of many more famous generals.

Merritt, Wesley

(1834–1910) Federal
Senior position: Division commander, Army of the
    Potomac
Final rank: Major General

Milroy, Robert H.

(1816–1890) Federal
Senior position: Division commander, Army of the
    Potomac
Final rank: Major General

When war began, Merritt was a lieutenant of dragoons in Utah. With an 1862 promotion, he and George Armstrong Custer were raised from captain directly to general. Merritt commanded troops at every significant eastern battle—Chancellorsville, Gettysburg, Cold Harbor—and was present at Appomattox. Later, Merritt fought Indians on the frontier and in the Philippines during the Spanish-American War.

An inquiry was required to clear the fractious Milroy for his defeat at Second Winchester. There, when he refused to abandon his fortifications, Ewell's corps, marching toward Gettysburg, overwhelmed his 6,900 men. A year later, Milroy ordered a disastrous cavalry charge, resulting in heavy losses. The one-time frontiersman, farmer, Indian agent, and soldier resigned his commission after Lee's surrender.

Above: Merritt was elevated along with Custer as a "boy general" of the Union cavalry.

Above: Milroy imposed a draconian regime on the Shenendoah Valley in 1863..

Morgan, John Hunt

(1825–1864) Confederate
Senior position: Commander,
 Department of Southwest
 Virginia
Final rank: Brigadier General

Above: Morgan was unsurpassed as a cavalry hero of the South, until he rode his command to oblivion in Ohio.

Born in Huntsville, Alabama, Morgan attracted trouble wherever he went. In 1842, while suspended from Transylvania College, Kentucky, for fighting, Morgan joined the army as lieutenant of volunteers. After the Mexican War he returned to Lexington, Kentucky, bought a hemp mill, and raised a militia company. Commissioned captain in September 1861 with a squadron of scouts, Morgan quickly became one of the South's legendary cavalry commanders. He led the 2nd Kentucky Cavalry at Shiloh and in December 1862, earned promotion to brigadier general. By then, he had become a famous raider known throughout Kentucky.

On October 17, 1862, Morgan led his cavalry around Federal lines on a sixteen-day ramble with two cavalry regiments and a battalion, which disrupted railroads, supply lines, and communications in more than a dozen cities. Morgan's first stop included his hometown of Lexington, after which he began a wide sweep west and south. The raid occurred so unexpectedly that Federal pursuit never got underway until the raid had ended. Although a minor operation, the Federals now realized that trouble in Kentucky had not ended.

Five months later Morgan conducted a "Christmas" raid. With a cavalry division of 3,100 men he crossed the Cumberland River from Tennessee into Kentucky and shut down the Federal lifeline by breaking up the Louisville & Nashville Railroad and destroying several bridges, two high trestles, depots, and water stations. Damage to the railroad influenced Rosecrans' decision not to pursue Bragg after Stones River. By December 30 Union forces began closing the ring on the raiders. After

capturing 1,800 prisoners Morgan realized that Union pursuers were on his heels and so slipped back into Tennessee.

In July 1863 Morgan defied General Bragg's order to operate only south of the Ohio River. He crossed his command at Brandenburg, rode swiftly to the outskirts of Cincinnati, captured 6,000 Federals, drew off 14,000 regulars from other duty, destroyed thirty-four bridges, and tore up rails at sixty locations. A strong Federal column caught up with the raiders on July 19, however, just as they were about to re-cross the Ohio.

Above: Morgan captured General Hobson near Licking Creek Bridge, Cynthiana, Kentucky, June 1864.
Right: Morgan's wedding in December 1862 was a gala affair, attended by all the top officers of the Army of the Tennessee.

After a relentless, seven-day pursuit, Morgan and most of his men were captured. Although he escaped from prison and resumed operations, he was unable to duplicate his earlier success. The hard-driving adventurer lost his life on September 3, 1864, during a surprise cavalry attack at Greenville, Tennessee.

Mosby, John Singleton

(1833–1916) Confederate
Senior position: Commander, 43rd
Battalion Virginia Cavalry
Final rank: Colonel

A small and complex Virginian who enjoyed literature, detested slavery and, following the war, became a friend of U. S. Grant, few would have predicted his rise to fame as the "Grey Ghost."

Mosby enlisted as a private, but soon came to the attention of Jeb Stuart and was promoted to first lieutenant of cavalry. He participated in Stuart's famous "Ride Around McClellan" in which the cavalry rode a complete circle around the Federal army. Mosby was captured, however, and spent ten days in prison before being exchanged.

In January 1863, Lee authorized Mosby to organize the 43rd Battalion Virginia Cavalry as partisan rangers. This became a regiment-sized unit operating behind Federal lines in northern Virginia—a region that some called "Mosby's Confederacy."

His harassment and elusiveness—picking off couriers, intercepting supplies, burning depots, and capturing Federal officers—so aggravated Sheridan and Grant that Custer hanged seven captured partisans. In return, Mosby selected seven Union soldiers to be hanged, although only three met that fate. In November 1864 Mosby wrote to Sheridan, who commanded Federal forces in the Shenandoah, requesting humane

Above: Mosby, at center with light pants and legs crossed, with some of his men.
Right: Mosby was commissioned a Confederate colonel, but led a band of partisan rangers that operated independently behind Union lines in Virginia.

treatment for prisoners. Mosby noted that he had captured—and returned—more of Sheridan's men than he himself had lost. Sheridan complied and there were no more executions.

After Appomattox, Mosby simply disbanded his rangers, refusing to formally surrender. Following the war, due to his growing friendship with Grant, he held numerous Federal jobs.

Nelson, William "Bull"

(1824–1862) Federal
Senior position: Commander, Army of Kentucky
Final rank: Major General

Opdycke, Emerson

(1830–1884) Federal
Senior position: Brigade commander, Army of the Cumberland
Final rank: Major General

As the Civil War broke out, this trained and traveled naval officer was placed in command of gunboats on the Ohio River. Recruiting in Kentucky, he was promoted to general and fought at Shiloh and subsequent campaigns with mixed reviews of his leadership. A big, burly man, he insulted fellow Union general Jeff C. Davis once too often, and Davis shot him dead in Louisville in September 1862.

Above: Nelson's brigade arrived at Shiloh late on the first day to scenes of panic.

Opdycke, an Ohioan, fought courageously through most of the battles in the west, but his crowning moment came at Franklin in November 1864. After serving as rearguard of Schofield's corps during its stealthy retreat from Spring Hill, Opdycke was disgruntled and placed his brigade in reserve. A few hours later, Hood's Army of Tennessee broke through the Federal line, only to find Opdycke's "Tigers" hurling themselves at the Confederate spearhead. After some of the most vicious hand-to-hand fighting in the war, the Union position held.

Above: A fiery leader, Opdycke earned an excellent reputation during the Atlanta campaign.

Pemberton, John C.

(1814–1881) Confederate
Senior position: Commander, Army of Mississippi
Final rank: Lieutenant General

A career officer from Pennsylvania, Pemberton fought for the South. Besieged by Grant at the strategic fortress of Vicksburg on the Mississippi, he was battered into submission, and forced to surrender 30,000 men. Captured and exchanged, he feared that his birthplace and the loss of Vicksburg would cause suspicion and so he accepted a lieutenant colonelcy of artillery for the duration of the war.

Above: Perhaps no Confederate officer was as despised by the Southern public as Pemberton.

Pickett, George

(1825–1875) Confederate
Senior position: Division commander, Army of Northern Virginia
Final rank: Major General

Above: At Gettysburg, Pickett's name became attached to the Army of Northern Virginia's greatest failure.

Pickett's career received a jump-start right after his 1846 West Point graduation when he fought notably in the Mexican War and again on the U.S. frontier and in Washington Territory.

Traveling to Virginia in 1861, Pickett was soon promoted to brigadier general. He dressed immaculately with long, perfumed hair and a waxed, drooping mustache while mounted on a sleek black horse. Wounded slightly at Gaines' Mill in 1862, he took a three-month leave of absence.

Pickett saw little action until Gettysburg and the ill-fated charge that made his name famous. Realizing that time was essential, Lee sent Pickett's fresh division—supported by several other brigades—walking in formation toward the entrenched Union line. The troops were mowed down, suffering more than 50 percent dead, wounded, and captured. Pickett never forgave Lee for this bloody tactical blunder.

At the climax of the siege of Petersburg, Pickett was overwhelmed at Five Forks. It was a pivotal defeat that unraveled the frail Confederate line, forcing Richmond's evacuation and Lee's retreat toward Appomattox. It was a humiliating defeat, because he was away from his troops at the time of the attack, enjoying a shad bake with other officers. By the time he returned to the battlefield, it was too late.

After the Battle of Sayler's Creek he was relieved of command, with only days to go in the war, and afterward he sold insurance.

Above: Pillow lent his name to the fort that saw the war's most infamous atrocity, after it was attacked by Forrest.

Pillow, Gideon J.

(1806–1878) Confederate
Senior position: Division commander, Army of Central Kentucky
Final rank: Major General

Pillow's friend, President Polk, appointed this lawyer a general in the Mexican War, during which he was arrested for undermining Winfield Scott. Appointed a general by President Davis, he quarreled with his fellow commanders at Fort Donelson, and sailed away on the night before its surrender. Found cowering at Stones River, he tried to undercut Breckenridge. Eventually Pillow was relieved of command and spent the remainder of the war in support positions.

Pleasanton, Alfred

(1824–1897) Federal
Senior position: Commander, Cavalry Corps, Army of the Potomac
Final rank: Major General

Pleasanton's father, Stephen, was famous for rescuing valuable documents, such as the original Declaration of Independence, before the British burned Washington in the War of 1812. Unfortunately, in the 1830s he was involved in scandals concerned with construction kickbacks from the building of lighthouses that prematurely deteriorated. Alfred was one nut that did not fall far from the tree.

With combat experience in the Mexican War, Alfred Pleasanton nominally commanded the Cavalry Corps of the Army of the Potomac during the Gettysburg campaign. Meade, however, understood the man's insatiable proclivity for self-promotion and politically undermining fellow officers, including his superiors, and refused to allow him to leave army headquarters during the battle.

Prior to that epic battle, Pleasanton's mounted troopers surprised Stuart's cavalry in what became the largest cavalry battle of the war, at Brandy Station. There,

Right: Pleasanton began the war with a difficult job, commanding Union cavalry against Confederate counterparts, who were initially far superior.

Polk, Leonidas

(1806–1864) Confederate
Senior position: Corps commander, Army of Tennessee
Final rank: Lieutenant General

Above: Though eventually exiled from the Army of the Potomac, Pleasanton continued to earn success in the Trans-Mississippi theater.
Left: Major General Alfred Pleasanton (right) sits with General George Armstrong Custer, whose flamboyant uniform might give the impression that it was he who was the senior officer rather than (correctly) the other way round!

leading a force of 10,000, Pleasanton's troops surprised the "flower of the Confederacy" and, matching the formerly dominant Southern cavalry in initiative, determination, and tactics, the Union cavalry "came of age."

By 1863, however, Pleasanton's senior officers had come to understand his inflated reports of his own performance and he was gradually shunted aside. In 1864 he was transferred to the Trans-Mississippi Theater, where he defeated Sterling Price in several key battles, effectively ending the war in the west. Passed over for promotion, he eventually resigned from the army.

Above: Polk, a bishop, was well loved by his troops, if not his superiors. He died when a lucky Union cannon shot near Atlanta hit him square in the chest.

Born in North Carolina, Polk graduated from the U.S. Military Academy before becoming an Episcopal minister. In spite of his lack of military experience, when war loomed, Jefferson Davis prevailed upon him to accept a commission as a major general to command the area between the Mississippi and Tennessee Rivers.

Though Kentucky had declared its neutrality, Polk feared the state would become a haven for Federal forces and sent an army to occupy Columbus, a small railroad nexus on the Mississippi River. Having fortified a commanding bluff overlooking the river, and stretching a great chain from one side to the other, Polk christened it the "Gibraltar of the West." Residents of the state were furious and Kentucky "went Union" in response.

Polk led a corps at Shiloh, and fought well at Perryville (where he accidentally wandered behind a Union line), as well as at Stones River. After disagreements with army commander Braxton Bragg, however, Polk was exiled to Mississippi and Alabama where he saw limited action.

Bragg's successor, Joe Johnston, asked Polk to join his forces with the Army of Tennessee for the Atlanta campaign, during which he commanded one of the army's three corps. In June 1864, while scanning enemy positions from atop Pine Mountain near Marietta, he was killed by a Federal cannon shot. Though never exactly considered a great commander, the Bishop's death was still deeply mourned.

Polk, Lucius E.

(1833–1892) Confederate
Senior position: Brigade
commander, Army of
Tennessee
Final rank: Brigadier General

In 1861, Polk, a gentleman farmer and university graduate, enlisted as a private in Arkansas' "Yell Rifles," and

Above: Lucius Polk was one of the gallant young officers who helped make Cleburne's division the most renowned in the west.

in a year became a general. Commanding a brigade in Cleburne's division, he fought with distinction until finally suffering a disabling wound at New Hope Church in 1864. Joe Johnston gave him credit for the Army of Tennessee's victory on that day.

Left: Pope arrived in the east full of bombast, but found himself totally unable to cope with Lee, Jackson, and Longstreet at Second Bull Run.

Pope, John

(1822–1892) Federal
Senior position: Commander, Army of Virginia
Final rank: Major General

Pope was born in Louisville. His father was a friend of Abraham Lincoln. Pope himself was a captain serving on lighthouse duty when Lincoln was elected president. Shortly afterward, he found himself a brigadier general of volunteers headed to Illinois on a recruiting mission. Although he was a West Point graduate, his political connections also aided his initial advancement.

Posted to the west under John C. Frémont, Pope spoke poorly about his commander behind his back, and took little or no action to follow Frémont's orders. Although historians tend to view Pope, through his entire Civil War "body of work," as timid and, ultimately, incompetent, he managed to beat Sterling Price at Blackwater, captured New Madrid in a surprise attack, and forced the strongly defended Island No. 10 in the Mississippi to surrender. There, Pope had engineers cut a channel that allowed him to bypass the island. Supported by Foote's gunboats, he landed troops on the opposite shore, isolating the island's defenders. The garrison of 12,000 men and fifty-eight guns surrendered in April 1862. Capturing the island freed navigation on the Mississippi as far south as Memphis. Thus, although he continually inflated his successes with personal posturing and bragging, Pope's early work was not without promise.

With his success in the west Pope was promoted and Lincoln brought him east to build a new Army of Virginia. He took over the army with great bravado, issuing a message that said, in part, "I have come to you from the West, where we have always seen the backs of our enemies; from an army whose business it has been to seek the adversary and to beat him when he was found; whose policy has been attack and not defense." Thus, when he so disastrously fumbled away the Second Battle of Bull Run and was relieved of command, he had few friends to come to his aid. Pope spent the balance of the war in Minnesota dealing with the Dakota Sioux, and then in Missouri. He ultimately served with distinction in the Apache Wars, called for better treatment of Native Americans, and retired from the army in 1886.

Porter, David Dixon

(1813–1891) Federal
Senior position: Commander, North
American Blockading Squadron
Final rank: Rear Admiral

Born in Pennsylvania, the son of a navy commodore, David Porter went to sea as a cadet with the Mexican Navy at age thirteen. Returning to the U.S., he attended Columbia College in New York, and then joined the U.S. Navy as a midshipman. Porter saw duty off Brazil, as a member of the U.S. coastal survey, in the Naval Observatory, and in the Mexican War.

When Beauregard bombarded Fort Sumter, Porter was forty-eight years old and a veteran of the sea. He joined the Navy's Gulf Squadron and commanded the USS *Powhatan* in the relief of Fort Pickens near Pensacola and in the blockade of Mobile.

Porter's first major assignment was as part of Farragut's fleet in the Battle of New Orleans, April–May 1862. Porter commanded mortar boats and steamers during the ten-day bombardment of Forts Jackson and St. Philip seventy miles south of the city. Ultimately, the Federal navy ran past the forts and the obstructions in the river, destroyed the Confederate navy and its ironclad ships, and then seized the city without firing a shot. Closing this port at the mouth of the Mississippi to Rebel shipping was vital to Winfield Scott's plan to strangle and dismember the Southern states.

Wounded during the amphibious

operations in Grand Gulf, Mississippi, Porter was successively promoted for each major victory. He directed naval operations up the Mississippi River from his flagship, the USS *Blackhawk*, including at the siege of Vicksburg. Success in the envelopment and battle

Above: During the campaigns for Vicksburg, Porter worked seamlessly in tandem with Grant and Sherman, who considered the admiral a friend.
Right: After nearly losing his fleet in the mud of Red River, Porter was no doubt happy to return to blue water later in 1864.

of Vicksburg gave the Union navigation of the full length of the Mississippi River.

The day Vicksburg surrendered Porter received his promotion to rear admiral. He was one of the first officers to be so recognized, as the rank was associated with European navies and ranks that could be purchased. He subsequently took part in the Red River campaign, where he almost lost his fleet to low water, and afterward severely criticized General Banks for the fiasco.

In 1864, Porter was given command of the North American Blockading Squadron. Historians claim that ending the South's cotton exports and its import of munitions was the Union's most effective way of strangling the Confederacy. Eventually, Porter took part in the capture of Fort Fisher in January 1865, which closed the last available port for blockade runners. Following the war, he was promoted to vice- and then to full admiral, superintended the Naval Academy, and took up a brief career as a writer.

Porter, Fitz John

(1822–1901) Federal
Senior position: Corps commander,
Army of the Potomac
Final rank: Major General

Right: Fitz John Porter was made a scapegoat by Pope for the Union failure at Second Bull Run.

Porter established a remarkable record as a corps commander until the war department transferred him to General Pope's Army of Virginia. Porter despised Pope and made it obvious to everyone. When Lee's army defeated Pope at Second Manassas, the general blamed Porter and charged him with disloyalty, disobedience, and misconduct. Sixteen years passed before another court exonerated him.

Above: Fitz John Porter (sitting in chair, center) fought extremely well at Gaines' Mill and Malvern Hill on the Peninsula.

143

Prentiss, Benjamin M.

(1819–1901) Federal
Senior position: Commander, District of Eastern Arkansas
Final rank: Major General

Price, Sterling

(1809–1867) Confederate
Senior position: Commander, Army of Missouri
Final rank: Major General

Prentiss spent the early months of the war fighting guerillas in Missouri, but on April 6, 1862, while commanding a division at Shiloh, he was captured while defending the "Hornet's Nest." When released, he served on the politically charged court-martial of Fitz John Porter before being placed in command of eastern Arkansas.

Above: Prentiss earned fame for his hard but losing fight at Shiloh.

"Pap" Price disdained war but joined the Confederacy because of Union policies in Missouri. He also disliked Ben McCullough, with whom he shared military responsibilities. After battling Federals in Missouri, Arkansas, Louisiana, and Mississippi, Price escaped to Mexico in 1865. When his personal plans collapsed, he returned to Missouri in 1867 and died impoverished eight months later.

Above: Indomitable, Price kept fighting, even refusing to surrender at war's end.

Quantrill, William C.

(1837–1865) Confederate
Senior position: Commander,
partisan forces
Final rank: Captain

Born to a Unionist family in Ohio, Quantrill discovered that stealing horses, gambling, and murdering innocent civilians were more exciting than his erstwhile occupations: teaching school and working as an army teamster. Although his partisan actions had little effect on the course of the war, his activities were widely publicized, perhaps because postwar outlaws Jesse and Frank James, and Cole and Jim Younger rode with him.

Despising military discipline, he organized "Quantrill's Raiders," simple bushwhackers who raided into the "free state" of Kansas. In truth, his enemies, Kansas' "Jayhawkers," were undoubtedly as guilty of crimes equally significant. When Union soldiers began executing captured raiders, Quantrill summarily shot his captives as well.

Quantrill is best known for his August 1863 raid on Lawrence, Kansas, which was perhaps in response to the imprisonment of Southern sympathizers, including relatives of his lieutenant, William "Bloody Bill" Anderson. At Lawrence, his men murdered as many as 200

Top: The sack of Lawrence, Kansas, where Quantrill's men killed every man, whether a soldier or not.
Inset: Quantrill as self-proclaimed colonel in Confederate uniform.

men and boys of military age.

When Union soldiers depopulated and burned several counties in northern Missouri, thus depriving his unit of sanctuary, the raiders fled to Texas. There, they quarreled and broke into competing gangs. Quantrill returned north and died from wounds received in an ambush near Taylorsville, Kentucky in mid-1865.

Ramseur, Stephen D.

(1837–1864) Confederate
Senior position: Division commander, Army of Northern
  Virginia
Final rank: Major General

Ransom, Thomas E. G.

(1834–1864) Federal
Senior position: Corps commander, Army of the
  Tennessee
Final rank: Brigadier General

Ramseur spent as much time recuperating from wounds as he did leading troops. Energetic and courageous, he was promoted to brigadier general at twenty-five. Ramseur fought in the bloodiest battles—Malvern Hill, Chancellorsville, Gettysburg, and during the Overland Campaign. When the Federals broke through the Bloody Angle at Spotsylvania, Ramseur helped stem the tide, saving the Confederate line. Always at the front, he was killed at Cedar Creek, Virginia, in October 1864.

Above: Ramseur was one of the toughest fighters in Lee's army.

When Lincoln called for troops Ransom was an Illinois surveyor and land speculator. Raising an infantry company, he fought at Fort Donelson and Shiloh and in the Red River Campaign. Often wounded, he died of dysentery while chasing Confederates through the South, famously remarking: "I am not afraid to die, I have met death too often to be afraid of it now."

Above: Ransom typified the kind of Union officer who had a background in engineering or other scientific skills.

Rosecrans, William S.

(1819–1898) Federal
Senior position: Commander, Army of the Cumberland
Final rank: Major General

A West Point graduate, businessman, and devout Catholic, Rosecrans began the Civil War as aide-de-camp to George McClellan in what is now West Virginia. Promoted to brigadier general, it was his tactical move—leading a brigade across a mountain to turn the Confederate flank—that insured Union victory at Rich Mountain. McClellan, however, took the credit and was invited to Washington to command all Union armies. Rosecrans went in the opposite direction, to the western theater of operations.

In June 1862, he was given command of the Army of the Mississippi. Grant had designed an offensive to trap Confederate General Price, but in the fog of battle only Rosecrans connected. Nevertheless, without support, he drove Price from the field—only to be criticized for not effectively following and destroying the Rebel army.

Rosecrans next defeated Confederate General van Dorn in the vicious two-day Battle of Corinth, where van Dorn's troops repeatedly assaulted Rosecrans' positions. Again he displeased Grant by failing to follow up his victory, and the remnants of van Dorn's army escaped. Still, Rosecrans was next given the XIV Corps, renamed the Army of the Cumberland. In December 1862, he marched against Braxton Bragg, stationed near Murfreesboro, Tennessee. In the Battle of Stones River—in terms of casualty percentage the bloodiest battle of the war—his right wing was surprised and driven back; however, he was able to hold on against further Confederate assaults. This earned a letter of thanks from Lincoln: "You gave us a hard-earned victory, which had there been a defeat instead, the nation could scarcely have lived over."

During the following summer Rosecrans orchestrated a masterful series of maneuvers to turn Bragg out of Tennessee. However, at Chickamauga in northern Georgia, the reinforced Confederates turned on him. Rosecrans, who stuttered in difficult situations, issued faulty orders that left a gap on his right. Confederates poured through and routed half his army, which escaped total disaster only because George Thomas was able to stand firm on the left. Rosecrans retreated to Chattanooga, whereupon Bragg occupied the heights around the city, trapping him and his men. Grant, who had recently been promoted to command all armies in the west, summarily replaced him with Thomas.

Effectively sidelined during the balance of the war, Rosecrans resigned his commission in 1867. He occupied the remainder of his life in politics and business.

Rosser, Thomas L.

(1836–1910) Confederate
Senior position: Division commander, Army of Northern
   Virginia
Final rank: Major General

Ruger, Thomas H.

(1833–1907) Federal
Senior position: Division commander, Army of the Ohio
Final rank: Major General

Wounded seriously on multiple occasions, Rosser was a supremely competent all-purpose leader, commanding artillery, infantry, and cavalry. Fighting from the first Battle of Manassas through Appomattox, he refused to surrender and, attempting to reach Johnston's army, fought for another month. Following the war he became a business executive and served briefly in the Spanish-American War in 1898.

Above: Rosser fought against his pre-war friend, George Custer, in several cavalry clashes in Virginia.

Few men participated in as many great battles as Ruger, who graduated third in his class from West Point. He fought in the Shenendoah Valley, at Antietam and at Gettysburg, then moved west to participate in the Atlanta campaign, won honors at Franklin, fought at Nashville, then transferred to North Carolina for the last battles against Joe Johnston.

Above: After the war, Ruger commanded the Department of the South and served as superintendent of West Point.

Schofield, John M.

(1831–1906) Federal
Senior position: Commander, Army of the Ohio
Final rank: Major General

Thirty-one years after the Battle of Wilson's Creek, Missouri, Schofield was awarded the Congressional Medal of Honor for "conspicuous gallantry" during that action. But by then he had seen far more momentous events in the Civil War.

After a series of assignments west of the Mississippi, in April 1863 Schofield was given a division in the Army of the Cumberland. Promoted to command the Army of the Ohio in 1864, he participated in Sherman's Atlanta campaign. After Sherman went onward to the sea, Schofield's army was detached back to defend Tennessee against the oncoming army of John Bell Hood. At Spring Hill, the Confederates got behind Schofield's force, and he was just barely able to slip past them in the darkness. The next day they attacked him head-on at Franklin, but were repulsed with immense carnage.

Finally joining George Thomas at Nashville, Schofield played a major role in the mid-December 1864 attacks that shattered the Confederate Army of Tennessee, rendering it a mere shadow of its former self. Afterward, sensing that there would be no more great battles in the west, Schofield requested a transfer to the east. He moved his corps quickly to North Carolina, occupied Wilmington, and fought through the end of the war with Sherman.

After the war, Schofield served as secretary of war, conducted several foreign missions, and was superintendent of the U.S. Military Academy.

Above: If not for Schofield's narrow escape from Hood at Spring Hill, Sherman's March to the Sea would have been considered one of the worst decisions of the war.

Scott, Winfield

(1786–1866) Federal
Senior position: General-in-Chief,
U.S. Army
Final rank: Lieutenant General

When war began, Scott was seventy-five years old and an American hero—serving admirably in every skirmish from the War of 1812 to the War Between the States—a total of forty-seven years on active duty. The only stains on his long service were his management of the Cherokee removal to Oklahoma (1838) on the "Trail of Tears," and the mass hanging of members of Mexico's St. Patrick's Battalion during the Mexican War (1847). In addition to military skills, he was a considerable negotiator and was employed to defuse numerous potential crises from Maine to Vancouver.

Widely known for his vanity (and girth) as "Old Fuss and Feathers," Scott was general-in-chief of the U.S. Army when South Carolinians bombarded Fort Sumter, although he recognized that advanced age prevented his taking the field. He developed a strategy called the "Anaconda Plan" to immobilize the Confederacy with a naval blockade; seizing important ports and control of the Mississippi River; and dismembering the rebel nation with surgical invasions. Although it was initially widely derided, Farragut, Grant, and Sherman employed the broad outlines of his plan with eventual success.

The insubordinate and politically active George McClellan—the general who always hesitated to fight—forced Scott to retire in November 1861, but the old soldier lived to see the Union victorious.

Right: Scott's "Anaconda Plan," though derided at the time, turned out to be prescient, as the war developed roughly along the lines he had predicted.
Below: Age alone prevented Winfield Scott from playing a more active role in the war.

Sedgwick, John

(1813–1864) Federal
**Senior position: Corps commander, Army of the
    Potomac**
Final rank: Major General

Sedgwick participated with distinction in most of the major battles in the east. Severely wounded at Antietam, he recovered and assumed command of the VI Corps. His battlefield achievements made him a candidate for commander of the Army of the Potomac. While placing artillery at Spotsylvania on May 9, 1864, Sedgwick was killed by a Confederate sharpshooter.

Above: Sedgwick's corps took the notorious Marye's Heights at Fredericksburg during the Chancellorsville campaign.
Following page: Men of Sedgwick's corps entrenched on the west bank of the Rappahannock River, early 1863, before Marye's Heights.

Semmes, Raphael

(1809–1877) Confederate
Senior position: Commander, James River Squadron
Final rank: Rear Admiral/Brigadier General

Semmes became a famous high seas commerce raider, capturing or destroying sixty-nine American ships. After the USS *Kearsarge* sank the CSS *Alabama* off Cherbourg, France, Semmes returned to the Confederacy and commanded the James River Squadron as a brigadier general. Forced to scuttle the squadron, Semmes surrendered with General Johnston in North Carolina as a rear admiral.

Above: The storied career of the CSS *Alabama* finally came to end when it met the USS *Kearsage* in June 1864.
Right: After Semmes ravished the Union's seagoing carriage trade, many companies reflagged their vessels under other nations' emblems.

Sheridan, Philip H.

(1831–1888) Federal
Senior position: Commander, Army
of the Shenandoah
Final rank: Major General

Above: Sheridan's relentless spirit contributed much to the final downfall of the Army of Northern Virginia.

"A brown, chunky little chap, with a long body, short legs, not enough neck to hang him, and such long arms that if his ankles itch he can scratch them without stooping," is how Abraham Lincoln was said to describe Sheridan.

This indeed was "Little Phil." At only five feet, five inches tall, the New Yorker was nevertheless filled with fighting spirit. After two years of Civil War, Little Phil and friends—Grant and Sherman—at last comprised the right formula for leadership, tenacity, and skill to finish the fratricidal war in which hundreds of thousands had died.

Sheridan's original post was to the U.S. Northwest. There he completed topographic surveys, skirmished with hostile Native Americans, and lived with a Klickitat woman named

Sidnayoh (called Frances by her friends), whom he failed to acknowledge in his autobiography.

Called east when the war began, he was assigned to Halleck's army in Missouri. As a captain, he immediately became enmeshed in army intrigue. Instead of sending him to an infantry unit, the cautious, suspicious Halleck ordered him to audit the books of former theater general John Frémont. It required the intervention of political friends to move Sheridan out of quartermaster and commissary duties and into the fighting. A year after going east, he was appointed colonel of the 2nd Michigan Cavalry, despite having no experience in that arm of service.

Barely a month after his assignment to the cavalry, though, Sheridan so impressed the army's division commanders that they petitioned Halleck to promote him to brigadier general. "He is worth his weight in gold," they wrote. Halleck complied and Sheridan's first assignment was command of the 11th Division, III Corps, in Buell's Army of the Ohio.

Although he exceeded his orders at Perryville in October 1862, on the first day of the Battle of Stones River he anticipated a Rebel attack and positioned his division to hold back the onslaught. His men withdrew in good order when their ammunition ran out. Sheridan's initiative gave the army time to rally and he was promoted to major general. His new command was the 2nd Division, IV Corps, Army of the Cumberland.

Sheridan's operations at the head of his division were especially notable

Above: The still-smoking Richmond, Fredericksburg & Potomac Bridge following Sheridan's Richmond raid.

Right: During Sheridan's Richmond raid his men left only scorched trucks and burned cars next to the shattered ruins of the Beaver Dam Station.

Summoned east to be Grant's cavalry commander, Sheridan quickly grew frustrated with the traditional cavalry roles of intelligence gathering, screening the army's movement, and protecting supply lines. Over Meade's objections, Grant allowed him to mount a raid toward Richmond. Although his troopers killed Jeb Stuart at Yellow Tavern, the raid failed and until Sheridan returned, Grant was left without critical battlefield intelligence.

Sheridan was defeated on numerous occasions by Confederate cavalry under Hampton, and his subsequent leadership in 1864 was less than spectacular. Still, he remained "Grant's man." Reacting to Early's activity in the Shenandoah Valley, Grant reorganized his forces and ordered Sheridan to stop the Confederate depredations there. "If the war is to last another year, we want the Shenandoah Valley to remain a barren waste," he wrote.

Sheridan had early success in the Shenandoah until Early surprised him at Cedar Creek. Away from the army at Winchester, Sheridan galloped toward the battle, arriving in time to help corps commander Horatio Wright

in the fall of 1863. At Chickamauga, the Confederates drove the right of the Union army, including its commander, Rosecrans, and Sheridan's division backward in disarray toward Chattanooga. Two months later, Sheridan's division was foremost in storming Missionary Ridge to drive the Confederates in confusion back to Georgia. Grant recognized that Sheridan's initiative was largely responsible for the victory and that the army was in his debt.

Sheridan has no superior as a general, either living or dead, and perhaps not an equal."

Following the war, Sheridan remained in the army. He served in Texas and Louisiana, showing little sympathy with those who were reluctant to acknowledge that a new day had dawned in America. He led the army through the Indian Wars of the 1870s, was promoted to lieutenant general, and ultimately, following Sherman's retirement, was named commanding general of the army.

Left: Sheridan's exhausted riders cross the Chesterfield Bridge to safety within the lines of General Benjamin Butler, May 24, 1864.
Below: Sheridan, left, in January 1865 with some of his subordinates: James Forsyth, Wesley Merritt, Thomas Devin, and George Custer.

regroup and save the day. In the following months, except for Mosby's partisan raiding, Sheridan's men eliminated Confederate presence in the valley. He rejoined Grant at Petersburg, harassing Lee's army in its flight toward Appomattox.

Sheridan demonstrated his aggressiveness by keeping his men close to Lee's faltering command. An exchange between Grant and Lincoln went: "Gen. Sheridan says 'If the thing is pressed I think that Lee will surrender.' Let the thing be pressed." At Appomattox Court House on April 9, 1865, Sheridan blocked Lee's escape, forcing the surrender of the Army of Northern Virginia later that day. Grant summed up Little Phil's performance in these final days: "I believe General

Sherman, William Tecumseh

(1820–1891) Federal
Senior position: Commander, Military Division of the Mississippi
Final rank: Major General

It has been said of Sherman that he never personally won a battle, but he won the entire Civil War. It might also be said that, more than any other man, he wrenched warfare from its lingering attachment to heroic glory beneath flying flags into the modern age of total conflict involving civilian populations.

An Ohio native, Sherman graduated from West Point in 1840 but saw little action before resigning his commission. He engaged in a number of ill-fated business ventures until accepting the post of superintendent of the Alexandria Military Academy (now LSU) in 1859. He deeply regretted the outbreak of war but was quick to offer his services to the Union.

At Bull Run, Sherman led a brigade and was afterward assigned to command Union forces in Kentucky, which was then under threat from the forces of A.S. Johnston. Sherman became unnerved during this period, and at one point an Ohio newspaper declared him "insane." He was transferred to Missouri, where Henry Halleck helped mentor him back to respectability. After Grant's victory at Fort Donelson, Sherman was given command of a division and fought at

Above: A voluble redhead, Sherman was one of the intellectual architects of the North's ultimate victory.
Right: Sherman surveys the scene at Atlanta. He became one of America's greatest commanders, a perfect complement to his friend, Grant.

Following pages: The Battle of Resaca, on the line of the Western & Atlantic Railroad, Georgia, with Sherman's Military Division of the Mississippi facing Joe Johnston's Army of the Tennessee.

Shiloh when A.S. Johnston launched the largest surprise attack of the war. Sherman stood the onslaught well, retreating only in tandem with the rest of the Union line. He had distinguished himself under fire, while he also began to forge a bond with Grant that would serve both men well.

At the end of the year, Sherman led 32,000 men down the Mississippi on transports toward Vicksburg, only to be repulsed at the Chickasaw Bluffs. On the next effort against Vicksburg, in spring 1863, Sherman commanded the XVth Corps, and after

participating in the city's investment, he marched to confront a Confederate relieving army, forcing it to retreat. After the fall of Vicksburg, Grant was promoted to command the Military Division of the Mississippi while Sherman took over the Army of the Tennessee.

In September 1863 news arrived of the Federal disaster at Chickamauga, and Sherman moved to help relieve Rosecrans' besieged army. At the Battle of Chattanooga he was assigned to turn the Confederate right, but failed to make headway

against Cleburne's division. Elsewhere, the Federals were able to storm Missionary Ridge, forcing Bragg's army to flee in disorder. Grant was now promoted to command all Union forces and went east to oversee the Army of the Potomac, while Sherman took over command in the west.

In February 1864 Sherman led an expedition to Meridien, Mississippi, in which he was largely unopposed but laid waste the town and surrounding countryside. At the beginning of May, in command of 100,000 men, he moved against Joe Johnston, with Atlanta his ultimate goal. Thus began month after month of daily battles as Sherman and Johnston vied with each other, the latter falling back gradually while hoping to extend Sherman's supply lines and find an opportunity to counterattack. By mid-July Sherman had reached the outskirts of Atlanta, and the Confederate government, frustrated by Johnston's inability to turn back the invasion, removed him in favor of John Bell Hood.

The aggressive Hood lost no time in launching three major attacks in eight days, each of which was bloodily repulsed. During August Atlanta lay under partial siege as both sides launched cavalry raids. Finally, Sherman decided to swing his entire army south of the city to cut its remaining rail links. Confederate counterattacks failed and Hood was forced to evacuate the city. On September 2, Sherman wired Lincoln,

Left: Sherman recovered from a nervous breakdown during the first year f the war.

daring strategic conception that proved the death knell to the Confederacy. Instead of confronting the diminished Confederate armies on the battlefield, Sherman had determined to cut through the heart of the South itself, forcing its civilian population to recognize the futility of further resistance.

In North Carolina, the Confederates hastily assembled a force to resist Sherman, but it was too little, too late. After a final battle at Bentonville in March 1865, and after hearing of Lee's surrender, Sherman accepted the surrender of Joe Johnston. The terms Sherman offered were even more magnanimous than the ones his friend Grant had offered to Lee. Though Sherman later coined the phrase "War is hell," and he had done as much as anyone to make it so, it was clear by the end that he had most fervently wished to hasten the peace.

Above: On his drive through the South, Sherman's troops wrecked Confederate railroads even as they rebuilt their own supply.
Right: "Sherman's neckties" in the making. His troops would burn Confederate rails, then twist them so they would be unusable until sent to a rolling mill.

"Atlanta is ours, and fairly won."

In November 1864, Sherman began his most famous maneuver of the war: the March to the Sea. Leaving George Thomas to hold Tennessee against Hood, Sherman took the cream of his army and cut a 60-mile swath of destruction through Georgia to the Atlantic Ocean. It was a

Sickles, Daniel E.

(1819–1914) Federal
Senior position: Corps commander, Army of the
   Potomac
Final rank: Major General

Sigel, Franz

(1824–1902) Federal
Senior position: Corps commander, Army of Virginia
Final rank: Major General

An utter scoundrel, Sickles was a philanderer and murderer as well as a politically connected New York lawyer. His headquarters, shared with Joe Hooker, was compared to a bar and bordello. Sickles lost a leg at Gettysburg when he moved his corps forward, disregarding Meade's orders. Washington friends awarded him a Medal of Honor, but Grant refused to restore him to a combat command.

A former German army officer, Sigel lured many of his countrymen into the Union army. At Pea Ridge he distinguished himself as an artillery commander but his reputation dipped while commanding an infantry corps in the Shenandoah Valley and at Second Manassas. An odd mixture of ability and ineffectiveness, Sigel never found his niche in the Civil War.

Above: Sickles' dispositions at Gettysburg remain an enduring controversy.

Above: "Ich fights mit Sigel" was a phrase proudly cited by German-American soldiers, early in the war.

Slocum, Henry Warner
(1827–1894) Federal
Senior position: Commander, Army of Georgia
Final rank: Major General

Smith, Andrew Jackson
(1815–1897) Federal
Senior position: Corps commander, Army of the Tennessee
Final rank: Major General

After suffering a wound at First Manassas, Slocum fought in every major eastern battle until after the Union defeat at Chickamauga, when the war department sent his XX Corps to Chattanooga. After refusing to serve under General Hooker, Slocum took command of a newly named Army of Georgia and led it during the March to the Sea and through the Carolinas.

Smith fought throughout the western theater, serving under Halleck at Corinth, Sherman at Chickasaw Bluffs and Vicksburg, and Banks during the Red River campaign. At Tupelo, he also became one of only two generals to defeat Bedford Forrest. After serving under Thomas at Nashville, Smith participated in the last western battle of the war at Mobile.

Above: Slocum and his corps were the first Union troops to enter Atlanta in September 1864.

Above: Thomas felt paralyzed at Nashville until he was joined by Smith's corps in late 1864.

Smith, Charles Ferguson

(1807–1862) Federal
Senior position: Commander, Army of the Tennessee
  (temporary)
Final rank: Major General

Smith, Edmund Kirby

(1824–1893) Confederate
Senior position: Commander, Trans-Mississippi
  Department
Final rank: General

Grant claimed his success at Fort Donelson was partly due to Smith's advice that he demand unconditional surrender. In March 1862 Smith temporarily replaced Grant when the latter was accused of drunkenness. While moving the army to Pittsburg Landing, Smith skinned his knee jumping into a boat. An infection spread and he died on April 25.

An instructor of mathematics at West Point, Smith became one of only eight full generals in the Confederate army. Experiencing battle from the Atlantic to Texas, this veteran of the Mexican-American and Indian Wars was starved of sufficient forces to maintain a vigorous defense west of the Mississippi, even though he scored numerous tactical victories.

Above: Grant may not have achieved high command had Smith not suffered an accident just before Shiloh.

Above: An able general, Kirby Smith's postwar detractors equaled his admirers.

Smith, William Sooey

(1830–1916) Federal
Senior position: Division commander, Army of the
   Tennessee
Final rank: Brigadier General

Stanley, David Sloane

(1828–1902) Federal
Senior position: Corps commander, Army of the
   Cumberland
Final rank: Major General

An engineer and bridge builder, Smith commanded an Ohio brigade at Shiloh and a division during the Vicksburg campaign. He later became chief of cavalry for the Army of the Tennessee but was badly beaten by Forrest at West Point, Mississippi. This led to a disagreement with General Sherman over his performance, after which Smith resigned.

Stanley fought in the western theater from the first major battle at Wilson's Creek until becoming chief of cavalry for the Army of the Cumberland. After participating in the Atlanta campaign he assumed command of the IV Corps, suffered a wound at Franklin, and received the Medal of Honor for personal valor.

Above: Would Sherman have halted at Meridien in February 1864 if his cavalry support under Smith could have joined him?

Above: Stanley's other actions could not match in excitement the twenty-four hours he spent at Spring Hill and Franklin.

Stevenson, Carter L.

(1817–1888) Confederate
Senior position: Division commander, Army of
  Tennessee
Final rank: Major General

Stewart, Alexander Peter

(1821–1908) Confederate
Senior position: Corps commander, Army of
  Tennessee
Final rank: Lieutenant General

After commanding a brigade during Kirby Smith's invasion of Kentucky, Stevenson took command of a division in Pemberton's army. Captured and paroled at Vicksburg, he returned to the field with his division and distinguished himself during the Atlanta campaign. He then joined Hood, fought at Nashville, and in April 1865 surrendered in North Carolina.

Above: At Nashville, Stevenson's division held its own, and did not suspect anything had gone wrong until it was nearly surrounded.

Stewart commanded the heavy artillery in Kentucky before leading an infantry brigade at Shiloh. He fought in every major Tennessee campaign and received command of a division in Hardee's corps. During the Atlanta campaign he took over Polk's corps after that general's death, and served under Hood in Tennessee, before finally surrendering in North Carolina.

Above: A. P. Stewart was one of the stalwarts who made the Army of the Tennessee a formidable force, despite problems in its high command.

Stoneman, George

(1822–1894) Federal
Senior position: Corps commander
Final rank: Major General

Streight, Abel

(1828–1892) Federal
Senior position: Brigade commander, Army of the
  Cumberland
Final rank: Brigadier General

Stoneman spent much of the war as a cavalry commander, but he also commanded a division of infantry in the Army of the Potomac. He is best remembered for his poorly conducted raids. During the Chancellorsville campaign he started late, disappeared into central Virginia, and bungled one of the most strategic cavalry raids of the war.

Above: Aside from his failed raid in Virginia, Stoneman also led a disastrous one during the Atlanta campaign.

This publisher was appointed colonel of the 51st Indiana. Given a brigade with the men mounted on mules, he was dispatched in a raid across northern Alabama to Georgia, but was chased and caught by Forrest. The Confederates captured both Streight and his wife, who served as a nurse. Sent to Libby Prison in Richmond, he eventually escaped to Federal lines and continued to serve, leading a brigade at the Battle of Nashville. In 1910, his wife, Lovina, was buried with full military honors.

Above: Streight joined a long list of Union commanders beaten by Forrest, whose partisans liked to call that action "a Streight flush."

Stuart, James Ewell Brown "Jeb"

(1833–1864) Confederate
Senior position: Commander, Cavalry Corps, Army of Northern Virginia
Final rank: Major General

Jeb Stuart epitomized the values of a Southern aristocracy for whom war meant mounted knights and chivalrous quests. He flaunted a red-lined gray cape and yellow sash, wore a peacock feather in his hat and a red flower in his lapel, and splashed on cologne before leaping into the saddle. It is thus ironic that a hardscrabble Michigan farmer, a man whose very date and place of birth are still debated, may have fired the bullet that killed him.

Stuart was born into an illustrious Virginia family and commissioned a second lieutenant of cavalry. Between 1854 and 1859 he fought Indians in Texas and suppressed civil disorder in "Bloody Kansas."

In 1859, Stuart helped (then) Colonel Robert E. Lee overcome John Brown's abolitionist force during Brown's raid on the arsenal at Harpers Ferry. Approaching Brown under a white flag, Stuart told the old raider that his life and the lives of his men would be spared if they surrendered. "No, I prefer to die here," Brown replied. Stuart then signaled the marines, who quickly overran Brown's stronghold.

When Virginia seceded from the Union in April 1861, Stuart became a Confederate colonel. With considerable style and a keen military sense, he rose quickly to brigadier and then to major general, commanding Robert E. Lee's cavalry.

In addition to scouting and harassing missions, his troopers screened the movements of Lee's army, thus confusing the Federal intelligence services. Stuart's cavalry performed brilliantly and on several occasions galloped completely around the Federal army, boosting the morale of the beleaguered Confederates.

Nevertheless, Lee's 1863 Pennsylvania campaign, which culminated at Gettysburg, was the beginning of the end. Absent on a raid at this "high water mark of the Confederacy," Stuart failed to join Lee in time to provide

Above: After Stuart's death Lee (despite being disappointed by him at Gettysburg) was heard to say, "I can hardly think of him without weeping."

information about Federal troop strength and movements. Lee's quiet reprimand, reportedly, "Well, general. You are here at last," was searing.

By 1864, the Federal cavalry had become the equal of the hard-pressed Southerners. When the Union campaign in Virginia began in 1864, Stuart's troopers engaged Sheridan's Union cavalry. At a crossroads known as Yellow Tavern an unknown private shot and killed the flower of the Confederacy.

Right: Marker at the grave of Jeb Stuart, as it appeared near the war's end.
Below: When Stuart's raiders rode around McLellan in June 1862, they disrupted Federal transport and communications systems.

Sturgis, Samuel D.

(1822–1889) Federal
Senior position: Chief of Cavalry, Department of the
    Ohio
Final rank: Major General

Taliaferro, William B.

(1822–1898) Confederate
Senior position: Division commander, Army of Northern
    Virginia
Final rank: Brigadier General

Having had both frontier and Mexican War experience prior to good service in the Civil War, Sturgis' commanders were certain of his leadership skills—until he was routed with great loss by a smaller Confederate force under Forrest at Brice's Crossroads, Mississippi in June 1864. Following this ignominious rout he was relegated to unimportant posts, and after the war he again served on the frontier.

Above: During his chaotic retreat from Brice's Crossroads, Sturgis was heard to say, "I will let Mr. Forrest alone if he will let me alone!"

Aloof but politically connected, Taliaferro served under Stonewall Jackson in 1862 and was wounded on the eve of Second Bull Run. Afterward transferred to military departments of lesser significance, he commanded the victorious Southern forces during the 1863 Battle of Fort Wagner (immortalized in the movie *Glory*) and the largest battle in Florida, Olustee, in 1864. After the war, he practiced law and served in Virginia's legislature.

Above: Taliaferro (pronounced "Tolliver") was wounded at Brawner's Farm, which saw the legendary fight between the Stonewall Brigade and the Iron Brigade.

Taylor, Richard

(1826–1879) Confederate
Senior position: Commander,
Department of Alabama,
Mississippi and East Louisiana
Final rank: Lieutenant General

A graduate of Yale rather than West Point, Taylor earned his military education by acting as aide to his father, Zachary Taylor, on the frontier and during the Mexican War. After joining the Confederacy he commanded the Louisiana Brigade during Jackson's Valley Campaign, winning distinction for hard-hitting assaults against Federal positions.

Transferred west, in part because of chronic problems with rheumatoid arthritis, he helped defend Louisiana against Federal probes, though his plantation was razed by Union soldiers in revenge. In 1863 he tried to relieve the siege of Vicksburg with actions on the Louisiana side of the Mississippi, but was unable to sufficiently distract Grant.

The highlight of his career came during the Red River campaign of spring 1864 when he gradually fell back before Nathaniel Banks' Union army, gathering strength on the way. At Mansfield (Sabine Crossroads), Taylor suddenly turned on Banks, shattering the head of his column. The next day, at Pleasant Hill, the pursuing Confederates attacked again, forcing the Federals to continue their retreat. At this point the entire Union gunboat fleet almosy became stuck by low water on the Red River; however, Kirby Smith deprived Taylor of sufficient forces that could have achieved one of the most spectacular victories of the war.

Promoted to Department command, Taylor's last action came at Selma where Forrest, covered in blood, rode up and told him the town was about to fall, thence Taylor fled on a railroad handcar through a swarm of Union cavalry. On May 8, 1865, he surrendered his Department to General Edward Canby.

Above: Taylor's postwar memoir, *Destruction and Reconstruction,* is one of the most elegant accounts from inside the Confederacy.

Thomas, George H.

(1816–1870) Federal
Senior position: Commander, Army of the Cumberland
Final rank: Major General

The "Rock of Chickamauga," as George Thomas will always be known, was a Virginian by birth. When he was a teenager his family was forced to flee into the woods when Nat Turner's slave rebellion swept through his neighborhood. Nevertheless, when the Civil War began, Thomas, a West Point graduate, chose to remain faithful to duty, honor, and country. He remained loyal to his oath to the Union, but he paid a price. His family turned his picture to the wall and never spoke to him again.

No armchair commander, Thomas fought the Seminoles in Florida and was cited on numerous occasions for courage during the Mexican War. In 1860, in an engagement with the Comanches in Texas, he was struck in the chest by an arrow, but pulled it out himself, and after a surgeon dressed the wound, continued to fight.

Thomas' first engagement of the war was as a lieutenant colonel in the Shenandoah Valley, but he was quickly promoted and spent the balance of the war in the western theater. Arriving in Kentucky in early 1862, he immediately took on a Confederate army led by George Crittenden and Felix Zollicoffer at Mill Springs and whipped it decisively. It was the first significant Union victory of the war, and came just as Sherman had been panicking that Kentucky could not be held.

While commanding the trailing division in Don Carlos Buell's army, Thomas missed the Battle of Shiloh where so many other reputations were made, but participated in Halleck's tedious advance toward Corinth—which on the morning of the final, great assault, was found to be empty. Subsequently, Thomas was promoted to major general; Grant returned to command of the army; and Halleck was "kicked upstairs" to a desk job in Washington.

Don Carlos Buell now took over the Union forces in Tennessee, but his superiors were soon frustrated by the army's inaction and offered the command to Thomas. Characteristically, Thomas, who wrote no war memoir,

Terry, Alfred Howe

(1827–1890) Federal
Senior position: Corps commander, Army of the James
Final rank: Major General

Terry never attended military school but became an excellent general, despite having been assigned to incompetents such as Ben Butler. He rose rapidly from regimental commander to corps commander, and after Butler mismanaged the Fort Fisher expedition in December 1864, Terry collaborated with Admiral Porter and captured the fort in January 1865.

Above: Terry's greatest fame may have come after the war, when his column was the first to encounter the remains of Custer's command at the Little Bighorn.

relentless assaults by Confederate General Bragg, whose battleplan was to turn that flank. On the second day of the battle, the Union right collapsed under an assault by Longstreet, and Thomas had to fight on three sides. Receiving timely reinforcements from Gordon Granger (plus much-needed ammunition), Thomas was able to hold fast until darkness. When staff officer (and future U.S. president) James Garfield reached him with orders from Rosecrans to withdraw immediately, Thomas explained that to do so would jeopardize the army, and he refused until the units streaming past his position had regained a semblance of good order.

Garfield subsequently reported that Thomas had been "standing like a rock." Although he sought no publicity and did not engage in back room politicking, he became popularly known as the "Rock of Chickamauga," and was given command of the Army of the Cumberland when Rosecrans was relieved prior to the Battle of Chattanooga in November 1863. This battle was a stunning Union victory that was highlighted by Thomas' troops storming the Confederate line on Missionary Ridge.

After fighting throughout Sherman's 1864 Atlanta campaign, Thomas was assigned to hold Nashville against the Army of the Tennessee while Sherman marched

stayed away from politicians and journalists, and was loyal to his superiors, refused the promotion. Lincoln then turned to William Rosecrans.

Under Rosecrans, Thomas' skills as a unit commander flowered. He played a vital role in the victory at Stones River when he held fast in the center while the entire Union right folded. It was the September 1863 Battle of Chickamauga, however, that made Thomas famous.

At Chickamauga, commanding the XIV Corps on the left, Thomas again held his men steady under

eastward to the Atlantic. It turned out to be a harrowing campaign as the Confederates, under Hood and Forrest, nearly trapped half the Union forces at Spring Hill, and then again the next day at the gory Battle of Franklin.

When Hood pressed on to lay a semi-siege on Nashville, Thomas prepared carefully, and in two days of battle in the December ice and snow, all but destroyed the Confederate army. Curiously, both Grant and a deputy, Major General John Logan, had been en route to relieve Thomas of command because Grant mistakenly believed that he was not sufficiently aggressive in closing with the enemy. Instead, Thomas received the thanks of Congress. To his wife he telegraphed simply: "We have whipped the enemy, taken many prisoners and considerable artillery."

When the war ended, George Thomas retired quietly and gracefully. He had honorably and well performed the duties to which he was assigned. Overshadowed by the more public and outspoken Grant and Sherman, the solid Union general from Virginia ranks among the finest commanders to have ever served the United States.

Above left: The Battle of Chickamauga saw George Thomas lose his derisive nickname, "Old Slow Trot."
Left: George Thomas won the Battle of Mill Springs, or Logan's Cross Roads, on the Cumberland River in Kentucky, January 1862.
Right: Thomas became "the Rock of Chickamauga" after the September 1863 battle.

Toombs, Robert Augustus

(1810–1885) Confederate
Senior position: Brigade commander, Army of Northern Virginia
Final rank: Brigadier General

Upton, Emory

(1839–1881) Federal
Senior position: Division commander, Army of the Cumberland
Final rank: Major General

A fiery politician but mediocre soldier, Toombs fought hard for secession and wanted to be president. When Davis won election, Toombs decided to become a brigadier general. After Harvey Hill reprimanded him at Malvern Hill, Toombs demanded satisfaction, which resulted in another reprimand. Toombs spent much of the war grumbling about the government and later fled to England.

Above: Toombs' greatest service came at Antietam, where he held the Federals off from Burnside's Bridge long enough to allow A. P. Hill to come on the field.

Two months after graduating from West Point, Upton suffered a wound at First Manassas. Fully recovered, he joined the Army of the Potomac. At Spotsylvania's Bloody Angle he won his first star after innovating a charge by column instead of ordering a conventional linear charge. By war's end, Upton had commanded brilliantly in all three branches of the army.

Above: An innovative young commander, Upton continued to write on military science after the war, influencing a generation of future officers.

Van Cleve, Horatio Phillips

(1809–1891) Federal
Senior position: Division commander, Army of the Cumberland
Final rank: Major General

Van Dorn, Earl

(1820–1863) Confederate
Senior position: Commander, Army of the West
Final rank: Major General

Van Cleve fought in many of the major campaigns in Mississippi (Corinth), Tennessee (Stones River), and Georgia (Chickamauga). After recovering from a serious wound, he commanded a division in the Military District of Cumberland and later in the Military District of Nashville until posted to Murfreesboro in November 1864.

Above: Though wounded at Stones River, Van Cleve's most hair-raising moments probably came at Chickamauga where the Union army teetered on the edge of total disaster.

Van Dorn commanded several western departments and eventually a cavalry command. He appeared in the battles at Pea Ridge and Corinth and lost them both. He never lived up to the expectations of Jefferson Davis, who switched him from one duty to another hoping to find the right niche. Van Dorn followed a practice of performing acts that improved his publicity without producing any meaningful results. His lackluster performance against

Above: Van Dorn epitomized the dashing Confederate cavalryman, but was forced to pay a price for his charisma when a jealous husband shot him dead.

Rosecrans at Corinth and accusations of drunkenness resulted in an investigation that vindicated him of any blame for the Confederate retreat but left a black mark on his record.

Transfer to a cavalry command proved to be a better fit for Van Dorn—a small but elegant man who rode tall in the saddle. He captured a huge Federal supply depot at Holly Springs on December 20, 1862, thereby dismantling Grant's plans to assault Vicksburg. General Grant, apoplectic over the raid, ordered Federal cavalry to chase Van Dorn, into Tennessee if necessary. Although Federal Colonel Grierson and his units finally caught up with Van Dorn, subordinates refused to launch a night assault, so Van Dorn's men managed to return to Grenada in triumph at the end of the year.

Strategically and tactically the Holly Springs raid was a resounding success. Van Dorn covered nearly 400 miles in two weeks, inflicting casualties to Union forces in excess of his total force, and destroying 1,500,000 dollars' worth of supplies. Overnight, Van Dorn became a brilliant cavalry commander, adored by the ladies as another Nathan Bedford Forrest. On May 8, 1863, at Spring Hill, Tennessee, Van Dorn's philandering suffered a setback when he amorously "invaded" the home of Dr. Peters. The irate husband picked up a gun and shot Van Dorn in the back, thus ending the career of one of the South's outstanding cavalry commanders.

Van Vliet, Stewart

(1815–1901) Federal
Senior position: Chief
quartermaster, Army of the
Potomac
Final rank: Brigadier General

Above: Van Vliet, like Montgomery Meigs, was one of the unsung heroes of the Union war effort, which depended on logistics as much as on combat.

McClellan's chief quartermaster for the Army of the Potomac during the Peninsula campaign. When his brigadier's appointment expired in July 1862, he spent most of the war supplying and transporting the armies in the field.

Although a West Pointer with experience on the frontier, Van Vliet saw little action. He served as General

Walker, William H. T.

(1816–1864) Confederate
Senior position: Division commander, Army of Tennessee
Final rank: Major General

Wallace, Lewis

(1827–1905) Federal
Senior position: Division commander, Army of the Tennessee
Final rank: Major General

Never in very good health, Walker commanded a brigade in Virginia before resigning in protest at Davis' military policies. Joe Johnston lured him back into the army as a brigade commander because Walker was one of the best. After fighting at Chickamauga, he was raised to division command but was killed at the Battle of Atlanta on July 22, 1864.

Above: A fiery secessionist, Walker raised a storm when he heard of Cleburne's proposal to enlist slaves in the Confederate army.

Lew Wallace is about equally well known as the man who wrote *Ben Hur* and the general who couldn't find the Battle of Shiloh. Though his division was posted only six miles away when the Confederates attacked in April 1862, Wallace's men managed to march and countermarch until dark when the first day's fighting had ended. Grant never forgave him. Afterward, Wallace redeemed himself to a degree by stalling Jubal Early's drive on Washington, D.C., at the Monocacy River in 1864.

Above: Wallace's "march" at Shiloh is all the more curious because he fought bravely at Fort Donelson two months earlier.

Wallace, William H. L.

(1821–1862) Federal
Senior position: Division commander, Army of the Tennessee
Final rank: Brigadier General

Grant thought that this lawyer was one of his best generals. Wallace volunteered as a private in the 11th Illinois, but was elected colonel. Promotions came quickly following action at Fort Donelson. Cool under fire, Wallace was killed at Shiloh while withstanding Confederate assaults at the Hornet's Nest. He is buried next to his horse.

Above: Many of the defenders at the Hornet's Nest, Shiloh, were from Wallace's division, which fought on after its commander had been killed.

Walthall, Edward C.

(1831–1898) Confederate
Senior position: Division commander, Army of Tennessee
Final rank: Major General

Although he was not a trained army officer, Walthall rose quickly through the ranks. He was wounded many times, and his courage and leadership were evident in battles from Corinth to Bentonville. He defended Lookout Mountain in the "Battle Above the Clouds," helped repulse Sherman at Kennesaw Mountain, and later joined Forrest in the desperate rearguard after Nashville. Following the war, he became a U.S. senator.

Above: In whatever theater he fought, a more courageous combat leader than Walthall could not be found.

Above: Though Sheridan humiliated Warren at the end of the war, it was Warren who in 1863 helped win the Battle of Gettysburg.

Warren, Gouverneur K.

(1830–1882) Federal
Senior position: Corps commander, Army of the Potomac
Final rank: Major General

At Gettysburg, Warren saved the Union by recognizing the tactical importance of Little Round Top. A West Point graduate with superb engineering skills, he commanded troops with distinction, but was often deliberate when boldness was required. Just prior to Appomattox, Sheridan relieved him of command, an ignominious blow that he never forgot.

Wheeler, Joseph

(1836–1906) Confederate
Senior position: Commander, Cavalry of the Army of Tennessee
Final rank: Major General

An 1859 graduate of West Point, Wheeler saw his first major fighting at Shiloh where he commanded the 19th Alabama Infantry. Promoted to brigadier general, he was transferred to the cavalry, eventually taking over the mounted arm of the Army of Tennessee. Army commander Braxton Bragg evidently preferred the earnest young officer over such wildcards as Bedford Forrest and John Hunt Morgan.

During Bragg's invasion of Kentucky, Wheeler fought at Perryville in October and then protected the army's trains as it withdrew back to Tennessee. At Murfreesboro at the end of 1862, Wheeler distinguished himself by circling Rosecrans' Union army, burning or capturing hundreds of supply wagons.

At the Battle of Chickamauga in September, Wheeler's cavalry guarded the Confederate left and the next day joined in the pursuit, capturing 1,000 Union prisoners. While Rosecrans was cooped up in Chattanooga, Wheeler (who was known as "Fighting Joe," or sometimes "Little Joe" for his small stature) launched his cavalry in a raid on the Federal supply line in the Sequatchie Valley, destroying a gigantic train of 800 to 1,200 wagons.

During the Atlanta campaign Wheeler performed superbly while guarding the flanks of the Army of Tennessee. When Sherman launched two cavalry divisions into the Confederate rear, Wheeler pursued and demolished both of them, capturing hundreds of prisoners. He was then launched on a counter-raid of his own to destroy Sherman's supply line.

When Sherman began his March to the Sea in November, Wheeler's cavalry was the only part of the Army of Tennessee sent in pursuit, With countless skirmishes he was able to

Right: John Bell Hood thought Wheeler was unsurpassed as a cavalry leader, which is noteworthy coming from someone who also fought with Stuart and Forrest.

limit the destruction wrought by Federal foragers or "bummers."

Wheeler was promoted to lieutenant general in February 1865, though with the Confederacy's collapse shortly afterward the order was never officially confirmed. Following the war he became a lawyer and politician, and is noteworthy for being the only Confederate general to command troops in the Spanish-American War. The story is told that upon seeing Spanish soldiers in Cuba fleeing under fire, Wheeler yelled to his men, "We've got the damn Yankees on the run!"

Wilcox, Cadmus Marcellus

(1824–1890) Confederate
Senior position: Division
    commander, Army of Northern
    Virginia
Final rank: Major General

When Fort Sumter fell, Wilcox, a Mexican War veteran, was a captain in New Mexico. By December 1861 he was a brigadier general. He competently commanded Confederate brigades and ultimately a division. Later, he served in Maximilian's French army in Mexico. Wilcox was never wounded, but dogged by poverty, and was at one time reduced to becoming a U.S. Senate messenger.

Right: Wilcox played key roles at Second Bull Run, Chancellorsville and Gettysburg.

Wilson, James Harrison

(1837–1925) Federal
Senior position: Commander,
Cavalry Corps, Military Division
of the Mississippi
Final rank: Major General

One of Grant's most efficient staff officers, Wilson was rewarded with a cavalry division in the Army of the Potomac in 1864. Meeting with mixed success, he was then "promoted" to the west. During Hood's invasion of Tennessee, Wilson was easily brushed aside by Forrest, which nearly caused a disaster. But he redeemed himself by turning Hood's flank at Nashville. In March 1865, he led a juggernaut of 12,500 cavalry, all armed with repeating rifles, into the deep South where he finally defeated Forrest, seized a number of towns, and captured Jefferson Davis.

Left: Richard Taylor called Wilson's 1865 raid into Alabama "the best conducted" of all the Federal ones he had seen in the war.

Wirz, Henry

(1822–1865) Confederate
Senior position: Commandant,
Andersonville Prison
Final rank: Major

A Swiss emigrant, Wirz lost the use of his right arm in Virginia and was then appointed to command the prisoner

camp at Andersonville. The overcrowded prison suffered an extreme lack of food, water, and medical supplies, which Wirz frequently protested. Some 45,000 men were incarcerated there and 13,000 died. Wirz was the only man tried and hanged for war crimes following the Civil War, though his conviction remains controversial.

Above: Preparations for the hanging of Wirz. In his defense, Southerners pointed to Grant's halting of prisoner exchanges as the true reason for conditions at Andersonville.

Wood, Thomas J.
(1823–1906) Federal
Senior position: Corps commander, Army of the Cumberland
Final rank: Major General

Worden, John Lorimer
(1818–1897) Federal
Senior position: Ironclad commander
Final rank: Captain

Wood is best recalled as the division commander who followed a flawed order at Chickamauga in 1863, thus causing the collapse of the Army of the Cumberland. But this officer was also a decorated veteran of the Mexican War, served with distinction on the frontier prior to the Civil War, and was twice wounded in battle.

Above: After the debacle at Chickamauga, Wood stormed Missionary Ridge at Chattanooga.

Worden commanded John Ericsson's experimental USS *Monitor* and on March 9, 1862, fought the CSN *Virginia* (*Merrimac*) to a draw in the first clash of ironclads in naval history. Temporarily blinded during the drawn battle, Worden continued commanding monitors for the remainder of the war.

Above: Worden's wound during his battle against the *Virginia* turned out to be fortunate: he was still recovering when the monitor sank in a storm.

Wright, Horatio G.

(1820–1899) Federal
Senior position: Corps commander, Army of the
Potomac
Final rank: Major General

Zollicoffer, Felix Kirk

(1812–1862) Confederate
Senior position: Commander, District of East Tennessee
Final rank: Brigadier General

Unheralded today, Wright fought from Bull Run to Appomattox. He developed the defenses of Key West, Florida, and commanded the VI Corps, Army of the Potomac, at the killing fields of Spotsylvania and Cold Harbor. A superb engineer and commander, he was captured once and wounded twice. After the war, he worked on the Brooklyn Bridge and the Washington Monument.

Above: During Grant's Overland Campaign, Wright's skills were underused as his corps was repeatedly ordered into simple frontal attacks.

A politician and nearsighted newspaper editor, Zollicoffer may have served the Confederacy better had he never joined the army. Talked into commanding a brigade in eastern Tennessee, Zollicoffer rode ahead of his brigade at Mill Springs, Kentucky, to get a closer look at the enemy's dispositions, and was killed by a Federal volley.

Above: Confederate hopes to maintain a forward line in Kentucky suffered their first blow when Zollicoffer was defeated (and killed).

Index